CORPO̶_____

PRESENCE OF BODY
GENDER BODY

PICTURE PALACE

# PICTURE PALACE

STEPHANIE YOUNG

ingirumimusnocte

ISBN-13: 978-1-934639-06-1
ISBN-10: 1-934639-06-1

Distributed by Small Press Distribution (Berkeley, CA)
www.spdbooks.org

Cover and text design by Tag Savage
Cover collage by Konrad Steiner

Printed in Canada

We are unable to relive duration that has been destroyed.

GASTON BACHELARD

And yet it has not been.

I set out to write a memoir. A plot of originary relation, and at each corner, a church. Protestant, evangelical, 1980s.

One church is a building on Wadsworth Ave. Another is a radio station, and one opens onto a series of schools (elementary, secondary, higher). One is a governing body, and one is a think tank. One is Colorado. One is a marriage, itself having taken place inside another church (radio station, school, think tank, governing body, Colorado). One is a kitchen table. One is a family unit of four, the marriage plus two girl children. One is the father's workweek, travel, wages: church that supports the other churches.

One thought she-child could eventually step outside. She found she could not.

Instead she found it everywhere. (Repetitive arrangements with more than one side. Her own, and other's. The house, its content and structure. Governing bodies.)

But she couldn't stick with it either; couldn't "spelunk". Indeed, she couldn't see a thing. Couldn't see the lines connecting one corner to another. Especially couldn't see the lines connecting one corner to its opposite, or to the corners of other plots, churches, schools, bodies, states, marriages, tables, family units, travel or wages.

Nevertheless the attempt seemed useful. So I bashed it with a stick (keyboard). I couldn't see what I was doing any better than I could see what I was running into.

At the same time I watched a lot of movies. I watched some scenes of some movies over and over again, in order to perform alongside them. I slipped in through the side. I thought I might be able to see something this way. The various churches' near-total injunction against movies and television (particularly rigid in those last years before screens married the churches directly) left me not a little obsessed with the form. Watching what congealed there, of the order's dominance, a slivered piece of the whole, absent from my earlier experience yet ruled by it like anything else, I thought I might have a better chance of seeing.

Everything was that.

The memoir thing falls apart.

Things rolled past my face, one reel after another on repeat. The bodies of those I love came close. Some went away. Some returned. I, too, went away and returned.

Some analogies and symptoms presented themselves.

There was something vaguely golden about it. The edges and middle of the film either blurred out, or disappeared in a series of bright popping light.

Much like my singular experience of ocular migraine.

Scene from the first novel (can't be located): a female servant or
prisoner sits on the lap of Cardinal Richelieu

                                                       can this be right?
He "diddles" or "dawdles" with her while making plans,
one of my earliest influences.

Gathering all these scraps of paper
-ing -ing -ing
over the river

which is snow

over the river
with one pony              (          )

now with three hundred    (0.33333)

damage was done to the ponies
with ponies

a prologue, then
to the engine


                      *       *       *


what's *wrong* with you
it *is* a jpg
you *are* a program

(did you mean *the image?*)

go, and find every instance
(I'm *going* to)            do likewise

the thighs of the new display
in series production
provide crisp images at all times:

having a very intense experience
part of which was trying to figure out
which time zone we were in

it's possible
(well it's always *possible*)
to destroy

the dots finally darkened and going away
so that it's difficult          to step down
to step back as you're going

*RICK, YOUR PURSE!*

like in the movies          I would
it would be          written, I said
not love you unless

or make cruel, bad decisions.
and threw the pen away
for the marks it made

those were that, too
thou *art* that

all the –anol,
all the –yne

in a non-stick formula still casts

wearily     it will have to be done
in speed     and under the cover of lotion

much is lost     for the viewer, that is

when your foot
hits the carpet
take a hard right,
or pastiche

"who holds the reins?"     yes,
who does?

then the bars went up
there were five in all
there was so much

\*     \*     \*

the vintage youth
in which I want to love you better
in which the original
interior, image repertoire

of behavior
in a dog bowl, not done
downloading music

books on the revolutionary war
stacked up unto a glass table top
pamphlets smuggling bibles to China

no it was the iron curtain
and bibles went behind it

as a child beneath the glass        gazes up
above it gazing down

darkly
upon the glass table-top

it took so long to fall
and having given thanks, broke it

even now, tagged
taking it in rows
even if one does not

take, eat
this is my body
"broken for you"

with the pastry fork
with the violence of plows
with pastry
with slander
with theft
with false testimony
with lust

with fights and quarrels

it took so long
how else could it

\*    \*    \*

NOW WHY DID YOU HAVE TO GO
AND DO THAT TO YOUR EYE?

\*    \*    \*

I correspondent
so sarcoma

finding unseen messages . . .
preparing to receive . . .

a young woman is walking through the park. It's

high tech baby in tile          late and dark
you've got to see this          incident report

"Don't,"
an election

footsteps behind her

prone to     go multitude


                    *        *        *


it'll let up     if you let it
rip the thermostat          right off the wall

good for projection
on the bed flush left
blood blister
with a little torque          on the half shell

bad feeling splattered there
and in water that gurgled up
and in William's dream (could not be listened to)
and in James' dream (could not be read)

like a cigarette on film     in the new century
everything          over-indicated
fine

one, how a blister shows up on the screen
two, touched by a wand
three coins tripping from the lap, music

an image too

the bus, cinched    blasts
and hits the air: an image

little hairs inside the ear
direct this gist? in the lining of the bell            the paper
(can't be located)   where someone else said that
someone else said that,    so

where to place the mark?

in its tyranny
I breathe faster
get down on my hands and knees
yet what you've seen across the room
may fail to deliver

I mean, it seems to me, you sitting by his side,
"divines your little one on one"
it's nothing.

nobody ever said it would be comfortable
with a blister on the inside


                        *      *      *


so that it would not act out
it was "toyed with"            the image

doesn't suffer, it likes the way it looks
alone in the room

brick bloodied by its own color
or property
arranged in circles

left a mark.
what color.
in psychology

the name is legion
in panties
to be remembered as Nancy Reagan

hard with feeling, cleaning the house:
"You know you give good brain,
like you graduated from a good school"

in the sense of an organ
a hand-organ

all thought    exhausted
of course a container,      and when
breached          the body

that is
even harder to get supplies through

when            I did it
and when        someone else

*there's* the blue crayon of mystery              pretty much
the blue crayon of agony        and I'm writing with it

with what's attached        is what's teeming
with arms and legs        on the screen

with internal organs, you can't just turn it off.

wakes you up, demanding a password—don't take this wrong, but
I look like a man, or a teenager

> ...pleasantly hardcore

*    *.    *

"I don't even know if they're *alive*."
"They're *muffins*."
"Well, they're not *dead*."

no, I insist            they were *all* poetic
in their extra fine-tipped ultra available way

moving as they moved    with the money
from one form      to another

so that the server knows you are finished
so that it may gather children from the local disc

when is speech *that*      and not just in a bubble
when *art* thou?          acted upon

by another's        resolution
and where?

the vessel dilated, or broken.
dialed, or token.

havana of a reply
data or, no attain

no attainment

on the airplane weeping
to "Blanche and Stanley"

*    *    *

I'm pretty much covered in putty
in that picture
it's time again, friends
for little pink umbrellas

and if they should come
who should say how they go . . .

tinkling sound, as the shoes move
back, and forth

I could skate away on
this near-dearth of information

at what point in the line
of lines .
attacked by dogs?

at no point. for I so loved the face
I would make its image
favorite, the same I took
I would take                again

to bind it twice

I think now I must have been allergic
nobody told me you could be, to that

"it is interminable"         labor, or
"who is depth"

in the gaslight
I need everything from a store

"No, sorry, that's an error. *I want to obtain something of value*, which is
a struggle although I have the money."

I had no formula for this need
which is monotonous

don't let something bad happen to you
something bad has happened to you
something bad is happening

                *    *    *

I saw a child step
out of its generative, polluted surface

precious, isn't it
what the tub is for

his head hung
from the hand of a man on the screen
for a long time it felt
itself, its head

ruined from its body      its own body
hung from the hand of a man on the screen

for a long time it stayed there
feeling itself

⸰masturbating to your own (one's) text

•there is no terror like that terror
it rhymes with terror

                *    *    *

broken at once        all at once
the clothes drier the hair drier

# MOLLY: SHORT DECLARITIVE

thus I lay on the floor
and the forced air dried me
and here

before the duct, like an optometry test
administered in a theater
in "Old Oakland"

you can get 10% off your dinner

once it's gotten pretty          with a fifty
you think you might lose your job

to never identify with the gentrified     can only see
one's arms, moving at the very edge      except for when

overtaken completely.          tourism.             android.

on a train I fell in love with
was it a boy? with a girlish ass?
or a girl with a masculinist—

I'll never know.

( what are you gonna do.           are you gonna stay with me.
  will you take me to the movies.     will you tell me a version of it. )

"the truth" in a weekend valise
subscript that powers the page

ragged metric
yellow umbrella

cream-colored sleeve
from which the wrist emerges
attached to a hand.
its lethargic grasp of the camera.

I wore those lenses out.
really gave it to them with my vision.

here (points to forehead)
(the arms move in a circular way
to all four corners of the room)

CHAPTERS FIRST THROUGH THIRD

Things really are coming too fast now. I have to eat them. Make the exterior fun! For the slow death, the fountain of youth—I just lie down when it gets too hot in the home school.

I can take it inside, I'm curriculum. On my knees, in the opening, they measured the length of my skirt. I blow up toward my bangs. It's cool.

Mixed up with the crowd we rub her face in the snow. Then I can't breathe very well.

He's going to do this *every day until it melts.* We push his parts into the toilet or lock him in with the gym bags.

My Baptist finger picks my Baptist nose.

A string of private moments glistens across the canyon, turn one over and the snow falls on a Sunday morning in bed. There's a miniature bagel, in the hand of a miniature husband, reading his miniature New York Times. I try to get incensed but miss and hang from the suspension bridge by my arm. A bad guy comes along and asks for change. He says he's starving but I can tell he just wants booze. Another one reads to me from a book of philosophy. At last the Good Samaritan peels my fingers one by one from the rope.

When I fall I land in the guest bedroom.

When I sleep I use the same eye cream.

When they raise the organ from the hold, one baptism won't cancel out the other. It seems so obvious now—the week inside the week, the umbrella under the umbrella, the double rainbow. I can only crawl out of my hips so far. Or onto his shoulders in the pool to knock down a woman crawling onto his other shoulders.

I remember being happy all the time in the future of limited possibilities.

I say *I hate you.*

The fluid rushing into my spine snaps me back into the heroic pursuit of literature.

A haughty voice discusses the film rights to my highly unusual childhood.

1.2

Then as now, a lack of retail makes it difficult to walk from here to there. This is why we love New York, all of us who can walk with safety between its shops. Every shop has a shop. Every corner has a corner. Then, things were for sale but the outlet was removed. This made it unsafe, made it a business park.

Running through the alley I saw bits of my clothing reflected in window squares and the more unusual triangles of anonymously mirrored buildings. We knew how much it cost to do that to your car. If it didn't come that way to begin with. Seams in the lawn running between the park's buildings. From when it was just sod. It was dangerous. Climbing public art on the weekends. Anyone could be there. Somewhere in the park.

We circled back to the church after evening service. After Chili's. After Denny's I lay my head against the felt animals or the cool painted cement of underground classroom walls. Noah clung to his felt board as I clung to him, or the ark, and the person coming around my back.

The screen overtaken by panties shows the ticking hands of a cassette tape in my closet back at home, ticking backwards. Then there were pews. Now there is a formal apartment for visiting dignitaries. The furniture's so slick you could slip right off. I can hardly walk anywhere, the outlets have so much space between them.

There's not even a park.

Only the false one, with its merry go round spun out of shape.

At the service, seated in the middle towards the back, I am deeply unin-terested in my fellow audience. As much as they make it happen, we're unfairly limited to description. They remind me of this, being stuck in it together, with each moment's limited engagement.

Like them I am waiting for something. Something to happen. Some-thing to my person.

I resent the erosion of liturgy, a chorus projected on three screens. This is a big theater and there should be a big red curtain. But the ones with the lines, they speak and it still rings. You drop a line and you are eating marbles, gum under your tongue or soap—

One: our mother fell from the piano bench directly before the sermon and after accompanying the final hymn. She fell from her place on the program to her back on the floor. We were all watching. Like somebody pushed into train's way.

Two: the usher having a kind of attack in the entrance to worship hall.

No one's first thought ever went to mechanics. We waited a minute for the spirit. When they came with a stretcher we weren't supposed to see. Maybe then, if not his health it was the polyester of his suit that made me so nauseous? Burgundy it felt like defecation.

Three: it was raining outside when a man walked into the Shell Station and spit on my winter coat.

I notice these little rents in the fabric of our favorite dress but nothing that might be seen from the stage.


1.4

Seated in chairs along the wall, or next to each other on the floor, what rushes through us and over the sea wall?

*I begged you, some of the Colorado I was, to leave me.*

He's explaining the benefits of anxiety, on a national level. That it may bring one closer to the Lord. We confess our individual failures to understand beheading as it is reported now. This shared misunderstanding keeps me. I can't speak for him, though he has spoken for me many times before.

I don't want to remember Fox's *Book of Martyrs*. What I remember is the belly of a man cut open and stuffed with grain. Wild hogs snarl on the edge of the page. They're about to be let loose.


1.5

Years later I attend the introductory meditation. The room dark and the DJ gilded. Here I am. To do something with the anger-betrayal. I discharge feelings in the dark, set to music by Seal. Look around for examples. Excrete feelings into a handtowel as demonstrated by the leader. Among us they are touching our backs when we cry.

The most base music moves us *here* to *there*, rolling on the holodeck's illusion. All the while stranded in Marin County. Grateful not to be a member. Until the whole of experience is underlined in green. For a minute then I'm lonely. Who'd move to Germany and into the group's shared housing. Whose leaders would demand that we switch clothes.

After a few hours we're given directions to think. People pass back and forth, praising our lack of attachments. We are a hypocrite. We have returned from the sea to find absolutely nothing changed, the phone still uncomfortably hot.

We did not really go into the water, not even to relieve ourselves.


1.6

As in a still of Giulietta Masina's face twisted up. Peeking from the back of a truck in *La Strada*. Then she's left on the side of the road. In the role of Cabiria she keeps calling, without exactly meaning to, on a series of seemingly helpful persons. First with the social worker at the caves, then a priest who gives her his card, and most dangerously, the magnetist who humiliates her nervous system onstage. Which leads finally, or in part, to the second man in one movie who'd like to push her in the river and take her purse. That's why her face is pushed in so many directions. She doesn't know how to swim. *She lives the life.*

"Just like the cripple," notes Giulietta, after going with Wanda and the pimp and his uncle, after purchasing a candle and opening her face with each step up the stairs, after bending down and kissing the last elevated stone, after putting her lips to the portrait of the Madonna, "we're not changed."

Then she gets drunk off one drink and furious with the soccer players who keep knocking a ball into their group, it seems, on purpose.

1.7

You left me there, holding it, feelings *smeared* across the face of my companion.

A self-congratulating system.

From the top
things come, drinking water
to return what's in me,
*too fast?*

No way. I tested. It comes in well below the acceptable level. I called it *thought liquid*,

sent myself away from my task, said I was a scribe among the buttons. Said I was my own companion. Button, *we,*

stand around second guessing liquid as it gushes from a solid rock. But in faith you can breathe all kinds of gloppy fluids.

Now I am pulling things from the freezer, there it is again, frozen ground round turned with a wooden spoon. In a teflon pan. Oh *here I am, I have to do this.*

We agree the movie isn't very good. It doesn't matter. She can't stop watching. Even when she knows how it ends.

One: a guy gets defensive, steps back into a parked car and the driver takes him away.

I don't remember what it felt like.
I don't remember what it looked like.
I don't remember what you said.

Two: We see the curve of her back in that scene. It is a good curve. It is a *redeeming feature*. It gets branded. Then we're seeing it again, her back, we're rushing to the sink—handfuls of buttons—

1.8

I wake up in the silly part about circles by Isaac Asimov. Yes I am ashamed of us, for riding the same curve so many times in a row. I can't stand it. In the meantime I am reading. I find out that the second foundation wasn't hiding in plain view during that particular episode of galactic history, they were only pretending to hide in plain view. Really they were some-where else, somewhere even plainer, manipulating everybody's mind from across the galaxy. They were the ones who planted the idea about hiding in plain view. They used the part about circles to hide their idea, and so themselves.

But the letters, I understood belatedly,

couldn't be a sign                    when they came right out and said so.

They could only be a riddle, like behavior. And even I wouldn't know when I acted that way. Because I was a bad reader.

1.9

What is the chief end? What do ... how many persons,

dropped here, on my head

the devil made me say that.
Whoever doesn't like it can sit on a tack ...

But why *are* we here? What benefits *do* the called partake of in this life? A mapping of lines is the *only indication necessary*. Tell her that.

One appears on each face in the end, regardless of station. Actually, it depends a lot more on the skin's oil production and pigment than character. I stop for coffee in the town where I used to live and wait at a table for my phone call. I read a magazine. It makes me late. A woman in an article discovers at 34 how that which could not be more *herself* reflects least of all how she imagines *herself*. 34 is a good age to find out she can't stand it. While recovering from surgery, she develops an ingenious method of watching TV through cutouts in the cotton covering her eyes.

There's a buzzing feeling going back and forth in my chest. It seems to be on skates, or on skis and skating into a lift line at the resort, trying to get up speed on a flat surface.

The skiers stand in line and then, in twos or threes, shuffle into place and wait while the chair of the lift comes around behind them. It's never clear if they decide when to sit or if the chair decides for them. The chair knocks their legs out. Then dumps them off at the top. Then turn and go down the mountain. Skate to get up speed in the flat parts leading back to the lift. Shuffle into place.

The feeling makes me want to go check out the recycling bag to see how much beer he's been drinking, or into his email to surf the undeleted trash, or take a shower in private, or turn the TV on and see what comes and attaches itself to the feeling.

Marilynne Robinson writes: "it is religious experience above all that authenticates religion, for the purposes of the individual believer."

She doesn't write it as herself in a letter. The letter's not addressed to me. But

*I still get the message.*


1.10

This memoir's for you, it is always happening. Flags of stone cut from the very material we are climbing. Moss grows on the side of each step. Even along the driveway and in the concrete face of a woman almost rubbed the whole way off.

I think I am ascending this inconsistent output magnificently, if I may touch the sore spot on your hip. But when I reach the top, or what we're calling "the-top-for-now", it's a shambles.

You get inside and it's a *shambles*.

The brotherhood of their differences, their Bill Murray.

My dollar sucked up the chute.

It's beautiful here you'd like it. Next to the water there's moss and ruin and extra blankets but people are still sitting in the library reading O Magazine. I can't forget that jerk from *Vanity Fair*. A small sign on a big field, it says CLOSED. Now the rain is really coming, someone slides the sliding door so there's thunder too. Maybe she's reading O critically. I mock all thirteen phases of the new harmonic standard calendar guidebook I find in the library, but that doesn't mean I am uninterested in the common sense of physical immortality—a good salary—fire purification—the saints—full participation in democracy—the death urge—nothing can harm me without my assent—I AM ALIVE NOW IN THE WORLD—the purposes of doom—

A five letter name spelled out in stars.

*Oh gosh, do you remember who that was supposed to be?*

Maybe we should take away her sign-making abilities. So that where she walks along the beach, several sets of footprints may be seen but none of them hers. Her companion giggles. Don't these legs seem a little realistic? Still, where she walks she breaks no twig. Even the dirt fails to note their passage. There's no real track to follow.

So said and it's done, or unsaid and done, the tattoo she intended to get still labels the back of her neck FRAGILE. A postal service logo. Perhaps she has TB or a heart attack.

All the pains are yours now: religious, physical, having to do with the mind. Tender moments are the worst.

Two angry feelings bounce up and down in there, even when the tenderness is at its most beautiful, the entire room smelling of forehead. If only something could be removed—but it's all arranged and spread in a way that makes this impossible. You'd need a pediatric tool.

Throb,
throb,
throb,

and all the anxious membranes say, *prett-y pathetic*. I'm even having a difficult time exerting my reflection. In puddles of mud and oil, yes, but in the *reflection pool*?


1.11

I waited—it would happen when I stopped waiting—I forgot what signs are for. So I never got to go up. The best prayer with no words still failed to effect that inner change hover looked for in children.

Now all the time. I watch the crowd without rancor. The crowd restless. The moment of its happening invisible, this heaving one of our own onto our shoulders, propelling her— what? beyond the door.

All the girls in line for toilets, text messaging, anyone could be taken up at any time. We may have blamed their mothers once but that was an error in thinking. So what, there's a PR kit pressed to their chests, delivered into a million grey plastic inboxes. One of us is going up on the *covers of magazines*. Every day. That they still need toilets is mysterious.

Fleshy growth! Where your outcropping?

I shouldn't complain, graced late, when I least expected it. The first time, I arrived home from work and greeted the cat. *Hello Kitty*. No one could prove I was thinking. The veil just drew back.

Sometimes it streams—of course the revolution won't be televised! Not because the most important things don't appear on television but because the revolution will knock out electrical plants and the TV itself will collapse under the collapsing house. So John on the island of Patmos. I too have wanted to destroy people.

I don't know how to text message at this point and would be charged for it under the terms of my plan if I did. So the site of reception gets limited. Somebody writes about one thing over there but I don't see it for days even as it bounces off a satellite and into the heart of a personal entanglement.

Because I can't see! Or hear!

Hyperbole—melodrama—all around commitment something goes wrong on my face. Yes I *saw* the cat in the brand, I *realized* things about the song concerning the revolution, conceptual things—things may even have gone into my heart one Saturday night so long ago. Thing after thing. The Fillmore. You drinking beer. In the crowd, under the chandeliers, I'm moved in their place to another, speakers mounted on the ceiling at Church of the Nazarene. Speakers because they spoke to me. All those Saturday nights. Each quartet with its comedic gravel bass. I waited beneath them for something to pull me towards itself. Its semi-circle. Waited to go up, shot into the sky of off-white plaster. Pulled up.

Then hover against black mesh, a sign of my commitment.
Then hover against black mesh, a sign of its reception.

I worried about members of the congregation seeing up my skirt while I hovered there but maybe nobody would notice? This *miracle on another plain.*

The speakers were repeating bug eyes. I waited.


1.12

Time is kind of running out. It's say-something-vulgar-or-get-off-the-device time. But that sliver of tenderness prods and slices at every turn, looming larger than actual size, a normal hand that feels enormous upon waking.

Sometimes it seems I'm impaled in a freak accident. I've fallen from the 2nd floor of somebody else's dream home and landed on the sliver. It's pierced me all the way through. I go to pull it out and there's a freaky suction sound. *It's sticking out the other side.* I don't understand. Oprah asks after the reenactment how it felt to be impaled. "Well," I say, "There was a lot of pressure. But the baby inside me survived."

Other times I'm in the belly of your tenderness, swallowed by a whale, holding my lantern aloft. A great sea of bile washes up and over the monster's ribcage.

*Really in the crisco now.*

It's like this: I'm in a cavern with a sliver. How long can our supplies last. Be reasonable.

1.13

She holds the edge of her chair with both hands and waits for Venus to go into transit. I'm not going to call his name. I can hold it.

The internet sings while we wait. *If you know how to run, sweet Virginia, you should run…*

Of course I know *how* but I'm not. I'm not going to.

1.14

When you go out the back and down the stairs into the garden, you go down and down and down. This morning everything seems particularly still. Only the faded metallic pinwheel, placed ironically in the gate that doesn't move, or lead anywhere, is moving. Metallic with stars and stripes, cheaply patriotic, cheaply ironic, cheaply placed.

It's everywhere.

I notice the set pieces also flapping slightly in the wind. Otherwise it is exceptionally still.

The garden I intend is dark. It happens in another time. In the garden I'm getting everything I asked for but am still not satisfied. You think it goes down and down and down but there's a back wall and beyond this end a parking lot, some cars, a house on stilts.

You go down.
It's a shambles.
*Yes but it's also cramped.*

I'm getting there, in a million little ways, if that's the way you want it. Formerly attractive handtowels folded in an unattractive way. That pack of du Mauriers—*a hard time.*

Poor Thurber. Eyes almost torn off by the end of writing class. Everybody had him in their arms, everybody with the anxiety of strong guys. Me too. Let me hold a part in my hand.

I look up "comfort, held," related to holding, being held, mother, nurture:

1. vibrator
2. Tetris Challenge Hand-Held Game
3. a demonstration held against rape camps whose occupants sometimes as young as ten years old were raped by seventy soldiers a day tortured and killed

1.16

A segment wanders off by herself. To think about the Rocky Mountains, what are lovely, where the Columbine is state flower. Where once there was a branch now it's missing. Grown over, it looks like an eye. These eyes on all of the aspen. Watching her climb over rocks in the dark. Mosquitoes bite her face at the lake of early run-off.

Chopping wood in early summer, the truck got stuck in mud on their way up. The mother loads them up with logs and pieces of quartered log, which they carry back to the truck again and again until it's full. Sap in their hair and the crook of their flannel arms. They hate someone. Especially the log.

My pronoun was never a young naturalist and doesn't feel safe talking about these things, rocks, highway tunnels through rock, not granite, something harder, but still she does. Here is a picture of her and her sister in the quarry. They believed their denim shirts came from the store.

Now I know my sweater comes from people and I live in a place, wherever I live, I can't really speak of it. Neither search results, areas of deficient research in her personality.

There's only a nonexistent past to gouge, in which they drive through other people's neighborhood. Periodically she's sent from the van with a pair of scissors to obtain lilacs for the people's dresser. The people related to her who love the smell of lilac. Herself among them. In the era before search results. She leans over fences or disappears behind them entirely. In the pursuit of lilacs.

A compulsive desire for bad picture books.
A compulsive desire for lilac.
A compulsive desire for du Maurier.
A compulsive desire for facts.

I'm getting there, where you ask in the dark if you can hold it. *It's comforting to hold it.* A part of her. Turning we ask the same question of the one we're turning to, can I hold it, *I find this comforting.*

The exact opposite of those who lived in a glen but did not die in the disaster. Because there was no structure for the water to destroy. Everything wrong here becoming a disaster, that people are not sleeping in their own beds. I can't keep crawling into the hatchback at bedtime when there's a room in the house for sleeping. The ground a mess of betrayals I've thrown from the car but can't really get rid of. They're not even betrayals. *It's natural* I tell myself, the ground moves, there's behavior. *Every war story has a hedgerow.* This isn't a war story but the nacreous layer of war around everything we touch. So we can't know what we're touching. Where we touch it's war.

Still we have a low tolerance for conflict, but not that comprised of gestures, the skin voucher, this walkway coming to an end, another waxy chocolate, the city on a plane—*doesn't it remind you of Mordor?*

Coursing down her back in braids. This always stumbling forward, forward into the garden.

When I wake up I get some juice. Like everything it gives me a pain going down and also after it's down but presently I feel OK.

In my now week-old dream, the menus were fixed. In fact the dream revealed that nothing was wrong with them to begin with. We just couldn't *see* them. Because we couldn't see, the menus seemed to be missing, so we couldn't interact.

When I wake up they're gone again. I click on the pull down but nothing comes.

William Vollmann: "In those days you had to be careful what you thought, because your thoughts would come true. Nowadays you have to be careful what you think because if you think it, it will never happen."

When I wake up I'm seated in front of the computer on my wooden chair, wrapped in his burgundy sweater, sweating. Hair hangs around my face in wads of grease. I think about how I'm already *two days past* that memorable foot cramp in the middle of the night, when I seemed for a moment to hover. And then immediately we're going forward again. Going down. Stuck in this terrible forward.

There's a lot of little wheels scattered around the desk, wobbling and wooden and once they were attached to carts. They are *have-taken-me* or *taking-you-even-now* on tracks, carrying things, doing things the others find permissible, or admirable, on a loop, the carts beginning to show wear.

So I haven't been entirely true. There is some little momentum, what we get from going backwards slightly. As with leaning onto my abdomen, I achieve a perfect inner stillness. I go backwards, into the forward. The house is a mess. There's

a woman with a cane
pushes her way to the counter
a young man with an unpleasant smell
pushes his way to the door
the man behind the counter likes to know how old I am.

*Old*, I say, and look down to get three pennies from my wallet but the old man at my elbow has it already, making the change one dollar even.

Where the house is a mess I purchased a pack of Export A extra lights, the grey pack, and a square log of chocolate biscuits from France.

*It's a love-feast, isn't it?*          you got it

*another Sunday in the vale of tears.*

Where tenderness flares, when the washer is on, with flickering lights and sparks and a warm electrical cord. There are frequently blown circuits, three-prong plugs forced into a two-slot outlet, the use of space heaters, irons, hair dryers, curtains and clothes.

The warm electric cord burns off its own paint. What sort of disaster, this lack of structure—it's going to save them, isn't it? The terrible sound comes from two doors over. But is it electric?

The lights of the truck pulling onto the lawn frame them in a pose of telepathic passion.

She's on all fours trying not to think. She's having the machinery inside herself a few hours from now. His blood drawn at the same time. For now the lights of the truck on the lawn are frozen. Are frozen them. Trying not to think.

When will it end?

*It's Friday, but Sunday's coming.*

But Sunday's always coming, and coming and don't miss the Good Guys Presidents Day Sale on the radio *would you love me if* something about smelling bad. Overly smelled, touched, eaten and drank from the same cup. *I was down and out.* Guinness comes now in a glass bottle for the first time, with its same foamy head. He called it *mothers milk.* And then I wanted to drink back. I crawled up on the shore of the bed, with that old time religion. I could love you on a bus.

2.1

We shall see if a significant tonal shift has actually occurred.

"Come with me," he says, the part of her with a walking stick, pokes around in the ashes for a moment, stirs them and creases his handsomely crinkled brow, "it seems like more of the same." Some muttering from under his hat. A pronouncement is made. Bad reading or none at all.

"No," he replies, holding up the contents of her shoulder bag, "this DOESN'T count."

Here she is bound to her own word, pursued by a walking stick, she vows to do it again and again even with the covers up around her breasts like an oblong sausage roll.

For a tonal shift to occur a movement in the domestic sphere is necessary. "I consume yogurt from glass jars, therefore I have intimacy with my fellows!" said some several times in a row while he comes along behind nipping at her heels. He yells towards her ever-retreating back, "Liar!" and then "you only WISH you were a liar, the kind who knows when they're lying—" a pause here for effect, "LIAR."

Many things must be made new for a tonal shift to stick. She draws up a list:

1. Recipes
2. The type of food we eat
3. The locations where we obtain our food
4. Pauses (duation, shape)
5. Incidence rate of Export A
6. Phone calls (duation, shape)
7. Social engagements, individual and shared
8. The falling asleep process
9. Sleep (duration, shape, mood)
10. The processes and order of waking
11. Saturdays
12. Workload

13. Movies
14. Bedding
15. Flatware
16. Physique

Any significant change to one item on this list should be enough to alter their course from one loop onto another. "Is that all there is?" he whispers, "LOOPS?"

A kind of dark jello begins to drip from the tap. Working up to something grander.

Twin houses for each artist, and a rooftop bridge between them? No. Something more like the arrangement between Ashitaka and San at the end of *Princess Mononoke*. Ashitaka stays to help the townspeople re-build Irontown but San must return to the forest. This upsets her but he is very calm and says he'll visit as often as he can.

A rearrangement of rooms in the house couldn't possibly be enough. We can only arrange the inside of our house. On the outside we're arranged, part of another arrangement, on the block, our house with the houses, our cat with the cats, and an overpass on either end. Ourselves and the items keep moving across the overpass. Sometimes you hear a car up there crash into a wall, or another car. Sometimes you hear it skid to avoid crashing. You don't know what happens. You can't know what happens just because you hear things.

An arrangement of categories on a list? Not enough either! Especially a list that doesn't include drugs, alcohol or plainly sexual gestures. Like the houseguest who looks up and wonders aloud why she said what she just said, when it's the opposite of what she thinks. That's our list.

Alli Warren: "We are lonely insofar as (because) we are co-each-other."

Only, when drunk—something may come in then. Perhaps a little of him enters. Perhaps a little of her. Moving in a rush past things to de-vour other things. We speak in drunken behavior, drunken thought, Brian Wilson: "I am that, thou art that, all this is that" outside of all arrangements trying to remain in the house we can't hear the dualities go rushing out the hole blown out the side of a passenger plane—

the change in pressure would be that intense—

3.1

Here we are in the imperialist city. Again. Mansions all knocked down to keep the fire from spreading. Sometimes it just happens. The tone shifts. There's nothing you can do to stop it. Sometimes you can make it happen.

"It's weird," the torso of *Good Vibrations* coming up again on the computer, "how she comes in so strong" in its delayed reiteration, "and I wonder what she's picking up from me." Then it's the end, weeeooooooo alien locomotion pulls itself along, "gotta keep those loving good vibrations" manufactured, basically, "a happening with her" when it all came so *naturally* at the top—

I remember shoving documents into the trash. I remember I want to remember the bus. When it got dark, after the dinner stop, we'd pull out our sleeping bags. But you couldn't really sleep there.

Spokane to Colorado
Colorado to Spokane
Spokane to Oakland
Oakland to Little Rock
Little Rock to Miami
Miami to New Orleans
New Orleans to Oakland

What happened before what's happening. Which started in a city. I stood there once and let it push water onto my pants. I remember I said *I'm taking the bus* but really I waited for you to come in your yellow car. To come and retrieve me. A car named Stella, that she is all gone now, down to the last revolving cell.

It's not hard to remember San Pablo when I'm driving down San Pablo or an egg in an egg cup

a blood tangerine juice

those girls behind the counter were cute

in the rain I remember your credit card
in the rain I remember your red scarf

how at the party they had the same kind of hair. My sears action dress. My sears action pants. Riding the bus was a relief, when I actually took it, or walked along the roads it took.

I remember a box of steam around my body and my head stuck out the top. I remember I rode the same bus every day and never saw what happened. I remember "a woman I mix men up." I remember her running down the stairs. I remember him remember I have to—again—

3.2

Reason not to move. In a list, *what did I know*. What I didn't get by listening in.

What was I in public, anyways? By the highway, I having more room to spread, I with an adhesion, de-adhesing I from you—

Doing it in public with a pen. A blue, blue pen. I hear someone talking about small Oakland. His family grew up there. Charcoal. Where I'm sitting. Being left alone. By my own doing, I'm waiting

to see your face
to bid you goodbye

sounds like *I* under a brocade, more aloneness, why so being alone, why shouldn't this
I be even *more* like Jean Rhys and really why not *all the time?*

oh maudlin
oh blossom
and not usually so cheeky

Henry James: "I'm always considering something else; something else, I mean, than the thing of the moment. The obsession of the other thing is the terror."

Taking pictures of the bus from the bus I am leaving the streets and the shelves that were not mine, are not now, were for a moment under my spell. A shot of what's spreading. Passed through its own circumfrence and stuck to the walls.

So there's me, in Napa Valley. The perfect cuckold. I guess I wasn't ever getting over the objects I have lived with

*shocking things she saw*
*what she found in Michael's bedroom*

those pink dresses I loved
in the picture in the kitchen

the barber, the butcher, the grocer—
it wasn't a dress shop at all!

In the end a bed is a bed. The address pricked worse than anything, not back, no more thought, only liquid. Crawling around on the red carpet with a sponge. It and what it stood for, his face for a moment, by the lake walking on its legs, dripping down the inside of a glass, the glass tipping over, fell and twisted my ankle in the water, a body of knowledge only five feet deep. They come on the weekend in waders for its trash. I want to join them. There's a lot of trash in here. It's not something that gets done.

3.3

Previously, she could be heard humming this little tune:

*I'm through with meat*
*I'll never fall again*

He's shown up at her house, and not just to slip mail under the door. In the damp heat thrusting itself out each wrist, one fluid sac buried deep in her left side, another on the surface of her right. One lung heaves for news. Coughs up fluid in the shower. Squeezes material from her neck in the new bathroom.

She thinks he's not happening anymore, or it seems that way. The dangers of meat you've eaten in the past, still coiled up inside with all those maraschino cherries. Wearing a Mossimo T-shirt. Only in these and other passive ways does he continue. Except for their hysterics of exchange. The mail drips toward her overladen with its own watery, symbolic weight.

But he was an *earth sign*. The bottom of the paper bag gives out

damp, she

runs into the repertoire at full tilt, grabbing blue glass bottles off the shelves on her way in, well

*smash that*

I'll gauge you later


3.4

This quiet evening in my arms
where every part of the laughter at her expense
is part of the dreamer
everybody's Cassandra at the drive-in

terrified, she's still doing it
in the hills, you used to work there—he, looking down
through decorative grasses

as if I had been swimming in chlorinated water
for ever, for ever ever, for
*ever ever?*

I woke up with a headache. No
I've *been* awake the whole time
but it did jerk, is it
what? Can I really find it
anywhere? And what style does
with time-signature-time
syncopa-

San Pab-
      lu, lu,               lu-lu-lu-lu

reading it again—
did I say that was relaxing?

I got it, you're taking my gum
your gum now
told you about my boots, the boots
"they are your children"
the little thing that happened
before the end of
little things
so I could say

"Daddy"      "teacher"      "AC transit worker"

what came up in my hands
pieces of the hive
the web that freezes you
in place      PROMISES,
PROMISES: I was thirteen.
I guess. "Ribbling?"
I wanted it.
Actually. Precise V-5.

In my hands, this new style
started to rise
you were loser of
its being over
a lock on the kitchen door
speaking to the artist
I knew
the first time in six months
might be yelling
with my sizes!

35

I just kind of went off with the weapon
neurotically. "It needs a little fire" or
"it could use a little fire," quotes from the marathon
all gone now. Pants you purchased in walnut creek, citizens
no name
not just collecting
I mean to do
*criminal activity*

a horse attempting
to meet the level, horse attempting
to match the participation
and falling
from her place on the feedbag.

QUOTE – QUOTE
UNQUOTE – UNQUOTE
OF – OF

Father – Mother
No – News

What about Esalen?

Why my abdomen, like a queen
distended
in the invisible way, all confession
a magic confession, "In the tin with you I seem to myself
DISEASED"

in the tin I seem to myself
in the tin with you I seemed

Tiny Dancer – so much water - into the pines

*Cruise 2 much?*

public togetherness
and the desire to be "inside it"
please stop reading my email

oh no
my liking

MONEY
MOISTURIZER
MORNING


3.5

They lived through the breaks of science fiction, where it's the weather who disassociates. She's always with me now. I am supposed to take care of her. Get her face washed and into bed.

Like a good, firm tofu                                    WE CLEAN SKINS

cream comes at the expense of cream.

The needle that keeps skipping, or attempting to skip, back onto the loop it just came from—will she ever get used to that?

How his head continues to exist on a separate pillow. How could he have known to hurt her with some new green shoes. Something you can only pass back and forth. When Nothing On the Table Moves. Green, the most mysterious, face inside a face, of something soft and rubbing yourself against it until in a blur it breaks the skin. Then you are drowning in remembrance. In bad bad sentence. She lifted her skirt in a frenzy to show where they, and that time quite deliberately, opened the skin. To remove things.

You approach the room with your appointment but what goes on inside so rarely meets your expectations. Typically, it exceeds them. The pews were slick and dumbly solid at the same time. Neurotically wet, like the congregation.

Deep in her nest now, she's unbothered by moist bits of tea that stick to the lips, cigarette butts, a lady's writing table. She sits there trying to make sense of the sheers. DEVOTIONAL CINEMA she thinks without yet having read the book that bears this title, DEVOTIONAL CINEMA.

3.6

She thought this was the epilogue.

But it was not. Like Maggie Cheung *In the Mood for Love*, she guessed she had just been practicing. Like Maggie Cheung she wasn't prepared for how much it would hurt. But the colors weren't as bright.

With the exception of her curtains, the music had a brittle quality, the kitchen in the church basement wasn't big enough. It was serial, or there was a quality of being sequel but she never knew. She gave a little jump in her seat when the water backed up and gurgled in the other room. "The special effects are amazing," and they were, night after night gathered itself up. She daren't turn her back.

This problem of discerning feeling from behavior. Maggie Cheung talked to herself in lieu of a partner to practice with. Which was which? She turned her face. Drowsy sips. From a plastic thimbleful of grape juice, how communion was served, along with crackers on a silver plate. You could tip the thimble on its side very slowly until it did or didn't spill grape juice all over the lap of a flowered Gunny Sax dress, and if you did, and it stained, too bad because those dresses aren't even on Ebay now. It's better that way. Or it doesn't matter because that's just how it is, he turns and leaves Maggie in the alley for practice. We don't know when it really happens because the film won't say.

Common grade
but here standing up
near the ceiling
not interested in anything
this music
isn't right either
that you are always in the poem
this new male pronoun
hovers there—HE IS HERE
the way I used to be
calling out, displaced

Baby, baby, why have you
forsaken me?
I'm not depressed, I promise.
Let me come over!

The house grave without
a hotel room of bad ideas
or a list of them on the hotel stationery
I threw away but still

Feel like makin'
Feel like makin' lists
Feel like makin' lists with you

Self-portrait with loose hair
Self-portrait with cropped hair
Self-portrait with turtle

Self-portrait with bangs
Self-portrait with my red hair
Self-portrait in satchel
Self-portrait in boom
Self-portrait with her numbers
whatever that means. Rising, ash, eat, air, etc.

Someone should take the internet away from me
for a little while
and I'll just lie down over here
in self-portrait with internet.

The great thing about being me is
all these icicles stuck in my face,
the letter m I guess
has a lot of interesting curves
whereas I have these stick-like qualities
for a second at least
while he rode away on his bike
I lodged in my own side
like a stick. The letter m has a pillow.
The ideal image of myself in the kitchen
where Julianne Moore's mother comes in
and out like an imaginary friend.

So the phone rings
and there is art on the wall. He wanted me to
feel like Uma Thurman
I think. Compliancy in a boat
and swimming along like a dog next to it
with Uma Thurman's yellow suit
in my mouth. I felt like that. Shrugged.
It's not too private. Once you've been stripped
of your rubber suit. Then you just hang out
in the freezer while he hates you

*　　*　　*

Like at tour's end
or when the sound cuts out
in her headset, and she's singing a cappella
for I am not driving
or walking to the store.
Lines driven wildly into the next line
a body turning on the bed crashes
and suffers. At the party
of engaged opposites.

Often, while watching this,
I was scared and bored at the same time.

*　　*　　*

I lean up to touch you again and again
on the face. Deity. I do not want to defile you
but I have to process. I promise
you don't have to find new friends.
Today's date is—how I delete
the draft. To anyone. You are over there
and she I avatar hazes the field

to anyone. You are over there and she
I avatar hazes the field:

my wife, my life, etc.

How could I not love them?
on the Stephanie Charles Riviera
where everyone says I love you.

A man talking to a pole
by the lake. I have been here
for ten years. Talking to a pole.

A person should agree not to observe a pole
if they hate it. Respect may be a structure
of rhetoric, but esteem?

                    *       *       *

So why would I?

                    *       *       *


Supreme ethical horses
run across the sand
in Calvin Klein's underwear.
I'm with them. Always confusing a bucket
for a basket. What can't be established
by touch. Not even your own arm
will do. Always the arm
of the other in a bad mood, an arm feels
full of rejection and hangs limp
by the side, my arm would prefer
to be sort of wrapped up
and sent down the stream, it 'eddies'
and other boy names—

Message from the box says the slut is young
and elegant. In combination something
feels italicized here, but too weary even
to denote itself. The gamers love me.
And why not—again an emphasis
escapes hissing from the door—
there was going to be something
really magnificent about my hair
in pins, coiled so much and severe
with descending curls.
Like reading Benjamin.
Who the girls complain of

in their poems of complaint
that the younger version
appears on every syllabus

no ribbons, no sun,
no lace at the procession.
Colette as a schoolgirl in the night.

Something hopped over me right there,
and so it was
the breath of the holy
which is anything moving
near this slab of pastry

\*    \*    \*

Woke up with the bomb
went off. Don't let me run
out of Woody Allen. Everybody said
don't run Stephanie
out of patience with me Stephanie
they said take cover.
Person-shaped cement
protective device other people
had and had to show me
how to use, but I wouldn't. A kind of
cathedral, it could.... not go off instead?

And this would be for everyone.
Like summer camp.
A friendly, non-bomb moment.

On the other side of this I am calmly
cleaning the red carpet. Surveying
the nice wall. Granted
that our little hotel is dull,

and the food indifferent,
and that day after day
dawns very much the same, yet
we would not have it otherwise.

Coming in the door is bad.
After a while everything
gets better. If you could just
calm down. Get in the snow.

*     *     *

The cucumber was muddled—and so was I—
with this other language. It sounds *too*:
waking up naked and bleeding
and all your stuff is gone.
Then Madonna is mean to you
and you swear you only had cranberry juice
and you'll never go out alone again
or say that you're on tour
with Madonna. You're a dancer
and they have good bodies
write it down this clings
to the yellow notepad
and the yellow light
in the beige kitchen

but after a while everything
gets better. If you could just
calm down. Get in the snow
and stay there.

*     *     *

Yet there is a limit to how long
a spirited young person can be kept

in cold storage. If only Iris Murdoch were here!
We don't have to drown like this
in a sea-cave. She would make you understand
the charming scene of meeting one's brother
when there is no longer any resemblance
between us. Tossing on my bed of snow.
Where you hear none.
Moms in evening view
or the vacuum attachment,
women in the film
requesting permission to *moan.*
With my comma on the wrong place.
I won't ask for these
bad lines! Ten days long
and coiled in the bowl
to tell time like Murakami
dropping the orange, Susan Sarandon
and Tim Robbins, Tim Robbins with Tupac,
the one where they stabbed each other
for treatment. The point
deep inside my own now. Femur.
Flat storage, the four things
I can't give you anymore of
or the act of her imagination, on this day
I declare war against the love in me
bouncing in my head
and rolled away, yet trapped
semi-forever on the stationery from Cannes

\*      \*      \*


Beauty flaw, I loved you most of all.
And where I go to prepare a way for you
I am not ashamed, I'm talking about
a LOT of citrus. The phone call that can't

hold you down, waiting on it,
I don't want that blanket
on my bed anymore
or not for at least three years.
Wrap it in plastic
the wave says,
will he be at the party?
Or in fabric, picture on fabric
wrapped in fabric
won't depose the train
for it barrels forward
briefly topping 67$ on the barrel,
a symbolic value placed on what cannot be
renounced. The train chugs
its liquid diet. Forward, forward, forward.

You can't say he didn't warn you.
You can't say he didn't warn you.
You can't say he didn't warn you.

Yes with his trousers. For the way they fit
never stopped, but my clothes
stayed on doesn't matter
ever traverse the narrative
and hatch it? The white goo I mean.
See me, smear
across the face I loved, of our own
creation. Where you woke up and
"I didn't know where I was"
something in my mouth
or someone won't stop
placing it, whatever it, white
and stuck, sorry, in me

*    *    *

46

I do some stretching exercises.
With a little click
the outlines of this being
fit right inside
and are locked neatly away. Oh why
oh why. "Just the way
I like it." Still a dark and empty lot
runs along beside things
apartments for rent
slime from the talent
too quick to say
we are the same person
at the pay station
yet "I can't bear the thought
of being freed by anyone
but myself."

The missed image
draws no pleasure on the lens.
Broad yellow stripe
at the base of the stairs, yellow
t-shirt under a brown sweater
exhaustion after labor. What these men
or myself went through
while the sun sits on them lightly
and do the bad math
of how to get you back
but no completion
dares complete me
forced astride this theorem. Acting
too bright in the kitchen, commented
"brightly" by which I mean
I seem a little false. When
her baby wants to see the wheelchair
she said, all rude facilitation

crawling on the floor, and that
happened too.

You didn't turn onto Lester
a second before me. You are not
your car these days.
Tender scenes play out
without us. Friends say no
the light's fluorescent. Open 24 hours.
In answer to a dumb question
about lights and agency.
Feeling removed from our own shirts
even as we are inside them
huddled nets of the bar
candles hooked there
in their own candlelight
a cave, not a cabana—

I mean to do actual theft.
Until I am restored here.
Until I am in storage.

*    *    *


Waiting for something else to enter.
Superhuman kryptonite
calls the cat in
waits faithfully
in a funny outfit
still believes in tweezers
their effective strategy
his tail in my face
bump in the line of a hand

"little"        "it"

shoves and tumbles from the tube
so something else can
rubbing his nose along my arm
wet and alone, enter the stream
and then the heavens opened up
and water streamed out
paper blossoms rustled in the wind
in the artifice of the branch
still war
among its reproductive parts
when nothing outside can cure you
but everything's outside
nothing human alien to me
everything seen and felt included
everything alien, everything
I saw and felt
on the shores of the Superior
covers pulled up to my chin
Barbara Hershey in Beaches
was like that, life-throb
already ebbing away

I went out into the city
and lost you

\*　　\*　　\*

That there is one inside me,
dejected and alone.
In our municipal trust.
Alone in our bed
working on it, thought bubble
above the head of an aggressively virile mother
could not be split
"you could see it had taken its toll"

as stimuli, when the cap flies off
two weeks hence, his paw
on the pen
in the dream or next door
and my name liberally spread
throughout, though cramped, the poem
he brought to writing group.
Prompting a desire for many things but foremost
to show him this, in my mind then
embraced on the bathroom floor
without concession, the form
of our continued love and in excitement
made palpable, the woman on the bathroom floor
with the papyrus, I felt very sorry
and sad for her.


                    *     *     *


Staggering through the building
with a watermelon
having the feelings of a stone
on the bear skin rug

for an object which is itself
in mourning
"which suggests how much we
need the other's desire, even if this desire
is not addressed to us"


                    *     *     *


These little turbans on my toes,
they're for you, too.


                    *     *     *


50

Those were the days of Brad and Angelina.
No I feel nonchalant, "those were the days"
of Tom and Katie. Of Jen and Vince.

Of those were the days.

Rocker hubby Gavin Rossdale
Mischa and Cisco
Jude and Sienna
Heath and Michelle

Britney and Kevin
Jude and Daisy
Swank and Lowe
Charlie and Denise

Those were the days
Those were the days
Those were the days

We were arguing about the color. We were drinking beer. We were drinking coffee. We were drinking tea. We were drinking tequila. We were drinking watermelon juice. We were drinking water. We were drinking white wine. We were eating donuts. We were eating goat cheese. We were eating Lara bars. We were eating pesto. We were eating potato sausage. We were eating pupusas. We were eating okra. We were eating salad. We were eating yogurt. We were dancing. We were drawing windmills. We were getting too many infections. We were going to the doctor. We were going to New York. We were going to San Diego. We were going on a walk. We were going to go to Boston. We were going to go to Denmark. We were going to go to Iceland. We were going to go to yoga. We were going to go to dance class. We were fighting in the living room. We were hosting a party. We were listening to 50 Cent. We were listening to Aaliyah. We were listening to Amerie. We were listening to Baby Bash. We were listening to Bobby Valentino. We were listening to Faith Evans. We were listening to Feist. We were listening to Jay-Z and Beyonce. We were listening to Lil' Flip. We were listening to the Lovemakers. We were listening to Mary J. Blige. We were listening to Mike Jones. We were listening to Leonard Cohen. We were listening to the Stranglers. We were listening to TLC. We were listening to 2 $hort. We were listening to Tweet. We were looking at cartoons. We were looking at the illustrations. We were moving boxes. We were moving our car. We were moving the VCR back and forth. We were picking berries. We were proofreading. We were reading *A Lover's Discourse*. We were reading *Folding Ruler Star*. We were reading Freud.

We were reading *Fun in Games*. We were reading *The Iliad*. We were reading *The L=A=N=G=U=A=G=E Book*. We were reading *The Lives of Wives*. We were reading *Over-Sensitivity*. We were reading *The Poetics of Space*. We were reading *Povel*. We were reading *The Romance of the Forest*. We were reading *Steps to an Ecology Of Mind*. We were reading *Young Goethe*. We were shopping in Santa Cruz. We were sitting in the first row. We were taking medicine. We were taking a shower. We were talking. We were talking about hysteria. We were talking about lions. We were talking about poetry. We were talking on the phone. We were talking to the cat. We were wearing a green bandana. We were wearing a black slip. We were wearing grey corduroy pants. We were wearing a hat. We were wearing pearls. We were wearing a white suit. We were wearing a windbreaker. We were wearing a striped dress. We were wearing a yellow dress. We were on the bulletin board. We were on the couch. We were in agony. We were in Ashland. We were in the bath. We were in bed. We were in the cabin. We were in the car. We were in the classroom. We were in a drawing of the clouds. We were in Duluth. We were in the hills. We were in the kitchen. We were in the lake. We were in Los Angeles. We were in Orinda. We were in the parking lot. We were in the pool. We were at the bar. We were at the barbeque. We were at the bookstore. We were at the flea market. We were at the emergency room. We were at the hotel. We were at the movies. We were at the store. We were at the reading. We were at the party. We were at the wedding. We were drunk. We were high. We were separated on the airplane.

March 29, 2006

When someone has made you hateful. So we are still here it is happen-
ing. You are not going to get away stuck to me. In the plane there are
extremes of hot and cold. I am in the plane, climbing down into the
boom, feeling it for the operator. Where he is trussed I'm feeling Mary
featuring Method Man, featuring 50 Cent, featuring Brook, featuring
Jay-Z, featuring Sting. He lays on his stomach for the duration of the
flight. I am alone like him. "Oh! She's in the *imperial* way." So what I
put the image inside? That's what the image did to *me*. I stood above the
tank and felt it. I stood on tons and tons of fuel.

My maple window. My apple tree. My mind goes "Harvey, please." I am
fourteen years later. Wanting her husband from the OC who deflected
anxiety in a measured, gestural way. Sexual anxiety. The double shame
impossible flood of images. It can't be that I am climbing the stairs in
the past to your door. I am placing the key in the lock. I am not sure if
it is the correct one. I am turning the knob and entering. You are in the
kitchen. You are showing me your face. Climbing the stairs. Lying down
on the bed. Being covered in hair. The feeling of a tummy. Dissatisfac-
tion. What is not happening is happening. "I have to say all these dumb
things."

The flat lake. Didn't show its birds this morning. No rabbit. No kingfish-
er. Overworking the shredder. I was bouncing a lot of checks in 2001
and 2002. I was paying more for my PG&E. The flat night that runs all
day. "This isn't how I wanted it to be," as I worked my way through the
ledger.

"I feel terrible," I said to myself. Then I got in the shower. Then his
protection was taken away. The fragments, I think they came from my
tooth, taped onto a post-it by the computer. Until Friday when I find
out. Ripped from—"You can't hold me down" (Mary J. Blige). He is go-

ing across the city on his bike, she calcifying in his mind. He won't change his mind, you can't chay-ange me, etc. Or a follicle when the hair is straight. Or a follicle when the hair is curly. She can't do anything *about* it—he thinks terrible things of her for the rest of their life. Yes I'm sure. What a flimsy she when he was done with her. Cutting and pasting things into a document before they are gone. The images refuse to copy. Sense of something going down a tube over and over. Or a follicle when something is lodged in it. Or a follicle when something begins to grow in the wrong place. I heard it. Going. Sucking, throbbing, receding, about to explode in the tube.

The ducks fighting more this morning than usual. Nobody to talk with. So this is how it's going to be. No, how it is. "So take me / as I am / or have nothing at all / all or nothing at all" (Mary J. Blige). There are holes in it. "...my poor astral body! Punctured and ravaged as a slab of charred swiss cheese" (Dodie Bellamy). The boyfriend of a performance artist in Beth Lisick's memoir who has surgery to remove the contact lenses from his corneas. They were sort of fused there. Drunk for many days.

First I heard a violent rustling in the nest. A nest with distance. Then I could read it up close. I went away and came back. I kept reading. It was getting worse. Rustling made it seem disposable. Dividing and repeating nest. A nest you are turning away from in disgust. Turning back towards. He warned me the link included images of both. But I couldn't download the software. So I was saved from images of combat. There are two stories. I am afraid of taking off my boots. Peeling off my boots when there are scaly things inside them. My feet.

So that I could say the car—your car—it is my body. Not in extension but a manner of driving. "Is there anything in my teeth?" Don't look *too*. Don't look at my car. Something pulls my coat around myself to hide it. It is myself. The coat that doesn't cover. The schizophrenia of vehicles diagnosed by their erratic movement. Of the eyes. Shifting from one foot to the next while applying a liquid to the face, especially one that is medicinal or poisonous or magical. Driving a face with lotion forward relentlessly.

A woman drowning in the opening shot, stripped of identity. A woman drowning. Defined in the extreme. To the extent we care about water in our own lungs, we consider the unnamed woman's future. To the extent we trust her named later. Her dislocation. In nationalism. Consider the movie that would open with this scene: a woman drowning, the water she struggles in lit by flames, from a boat, the boat is coming apart, its pieces are catching on fire, they are casting light, where the bellows or a generator were applied. A movie that would fail to place this, all of this (with a broad gesture of the hand) in sequence later. Or of a child playing with her father, abandoned in a snowy grove of pines. Repeated later it is straight to video. Things will be wrung from us, the photo clutched by a drowning woman, carried across the ocean even while she is in it. Johnny Depp speaks in this film maybe three times.

Faith Evans learning from her mistakes but here not as things should be. We had got as far as play. "A great deal of repetitiveness occurs" (Erving Goffman) and "frequent switching...resulting in a mixing up of the dominance order found among the players during occasions of literal activity." Also stopping, redoing, the mixing of sequences, all of it continuing longer than would the actual behavior it is patterned after. Between animals. Where the signals are voluntary and involuntary at the same time. I don't choose Leonard Cohen, "its broken waist in your hand." Chooses me.

Heavy flow with intermittent nausea, as in vision. "In truth, when we turn our heads we don't see a graceful continuum but a series of tiny jump-cuts, little stills joined, perhaps, by infinitesimal dissolves. Thus our visual experience in daily life is akin to the intermittence of cinema" (Nathaniel Dorsky). Days later, still over-stimulated by the chocolate bar. Digestion. Interspecies play, a mink carried in the mouth of a bear. Is how we spent the morning in heaven. You cannot stay in bed all day. I heard a loud voice and the heavens opened up. I am balancing my checkbook while the Keyshia Cole album downloads.

All around the United States people all agree. Hills are the same everywhere. So we avoid them. I did what I said I would do. But because it was raining I had to go through the hills partway. Slightly ashamed of how beautiful I found the view from the top of Cleveland Cascade.

What I thought was Cleveland Cavalcade, a procession of people traveling on horseback, or carriages, or ships. A dramatic sequence. Or ashamed that I ever told Suzanne the lake isn't real. The water solid and clear. A function of the wind. The green all gone away. The lake had improved, been improved, gotten better. Recovered. I thought to emulate this, to throw myself upon the back, or mercy, of a hill as it rode by. Attach myself to some hidden but inconsequential cottage, so unnecessary it might rent for seven or seven hundred and fifty dollars a month. But with a security system of cars. To be in the bosom of a hill, milking its fat, so rich the double-paned windows wouldn't fog up. As if carried on the back of another, I would use a method of transportation in which truck trailers are carried on trains, in connection with something larger or more important than myself, aligned with an issue, gaining access to a restricted communications channel by using the session another user had already established. "Moving through its layers / moving up," I thought while descending the stairs, those like a small waterfall or series of waterfalls, "in the hall of higher education." As I got closer to the lake a downed tree. The same everywhere. Surrounded by yellow tape. The other trees had red placards, and these placards I saw had numbers and then I didn't want to get any closer. Not getting past pre-action anxiety. Because the next step is always behavior. Until then, and only for a moment, I identified wildly with Henri Rousseau. As a figure. Should I get a print? Can I know what I like to look at without identification? The negative kind. I am taking the French avant-garde by storm with my lack.

Avoiding. Making it seem. A stalker. With smells. And then you get flooded, there are shards in the drive. Not getting over it. Shame over having used a bomb metaphor for adolescent experience, sense of the self, or the self's momentary accessories, as a bomb. "i was a human bomb, a greased and mushrooming drill. the bus was moving into a black hole. i didn't resist. i saw his face and relaxed and left. i was gone" (Patti Smith). A minefield. My eyes have seen—the market. Deep shame of metaphor. Deepness of the lake at its deepest point, not very. Still, the intoxication of a girl or woman walking in the dark along its southeastern edge, under an umbrella. In a tailored coat. Counting down to sleep. Unsuccessfully. Easily marred by irritation. Forced into thinking all the time *This Connection of Everyone with Lungs* (Juliana Spahr). And not unpleasurably. And not pleasurably. But also thinking very hard about breathing like students at a boarding school might.

I can't do it in the rain, or "you just don't THINK you can," so the lake seems lost to me. All the ideas come from other people. Like a lake. I can see it, but I can't get too close. "Each of us carries a lake inside themselves!" That Colette rested in Balzac as in a cradle. Balzac as a forest for Colette. "Soldiers really are like forests, the men aching like wood to be cut down" (David Larsen). As if wearing a costume fitted with fur from the inside out. Everything's outside, everything's inside. Everything I know about King Kong I learned from Dodie. But I really can't get it, standing in rain on the opposite shore of glass. Things arrive. Things depart. I am among them, above the lake in a plane. Emerging from the fog suddenly, in the way of adjusted flight paths. A necessarily difficult conversation, but that it was undertaken at all. Because it is the only conversation of its type that I've known. *Your Body's Many Cries for Water* (F. Batmanghelidj). "You are not sick, you are thirsty."

Sleeping in a group, in the trash, with their heads tucked into their shoulders. That is how the ducks do it. The geese clean their heads near the jet, neurotically. Or one of them does while the others watch. The swimming birds peer deeply into the algal bloom and leave a trail through it. That the lake is endlessly available for analogy and metaphor. Is how it became a real lake in a real landscape. Full of trash and covered in a green film today, the lake is being discussed.

I was logged in as Stephanie Young. I was looking at photos and eating dried papaya, dried without sugar or preserving agents. My photos didn't have enough light in them. I had been gone for several days.

I waited, the program fetching messages. It would happen when I stopped waiting. Methods. "Lift up now thine eyes," with a broad gesture of the arm and hand, "and look from the place where thou art," the next seven words not included here are directions, "for all the land which thou seest, to thee will I give it, and to thy seed for ever" (Genesis 13:14-17). And so I had my expressive freedom. Was it worth it? "Let me work it / I put my thing down, flip it and reverse it" (Missy Elliott). Like dust on the earth, immeasurable. Like seed. Making me who I was. And who I wrote with. What I had not acted against. Thinking all day about action. Can't. How she wanted, I wanted, to know my friend's position on action, wanted that position to appear in the book, or sooner than it did, she was not a pacifist it said at the end, or I thought I did, want to know, but did not know my own. Positionality. So she went around the lake always half-cocked. Half-mast. Half a sandwich and cream of asparagus soup while she waited for the urinary analgesic. I was she.

That we could come of age inside another person's coming of age story, or come to political consciousness inside another person's coming to political consciousness story, haven't people been doing that forever? For instance with *Catcher in the Rye*? That is a terrible example. I mean *Little Women*. Like wearing a bear coat or "wallowing in its gorgeous syntax, like a hermit crab would in a particularly elegant new shell" (Nada Gordon). It was summer and the couch looked like black leather with black leather buttons. I cried. To experience the summer rain. With the little women. But what about discomfort. What about irritation. The necessary coming of agents. The couch was just a couch. It had buttons. The house was too strong a container. Bad religion in all the rooms. I seemed to be alone on the couch. "Ah - alone with my thoughts!" If only. There were thoughts, inside it, the couch, and the little women who had lain there before me.

How the ducks do it in the cold. I've got to be that slow. My human love must accommodate so much more, "that was way more milk than I ever thought I could accommodate." That was me once. Wondering. How does I not molest itself, standing there with water dripping off? Standing there in the shower stall, dripping, standing there in a compartment for one domestic animal in a barn or shed, standing there in a booth, standing there in a cubicle, at a market, in a pew in a church, in a seat in the front of a theater, standing there in a space marked off for a motor vehicle, standing there in a protective sheath for a finger or toe, standing there with sudden, unintended loss of power or effectiveness, standing there experiencing an interruption of airflow resulting in a loss of lift and a tendency to drop.

"who will include everything? / who will be the one expanding? / who will be the one expanding / to include everything / with no one to blame?" (Aaron Kiely) It started a year ago so it'll end a year ago. A year ago later same timing but the light is different. Doing it daylight savings style. Institutional style. The light is pervasive. And probably really the same. But something is still different. The new ducks.

Rejection dreams. *L Word* dreams. "The second season is terrible," I tell Cynthia on the phone, "but guess who watched the whole thing?" I feel I must admit to this next thing, but hasn't everyone fantasized about choking on a sandwich? In the kitchen? Alone. Even if you live with someone it could happen. Or a vitamin pill. L-Lysine, particularly large and grainy.

I thought she was methodically tearing pages from the magazine for a trash nest. I thought she was homelessly insane. Then I was struck down on the train, I was blind but I could see, the laboriousness of love, she was making a magazine *for* someone, free of advertisement. Not herself reading as she went along. Only tearing it into a new thing. Preparing the way. It seemed like love.

"Now I can see things for what they really are" (Madonna). But also "the more that I wait the more time that I waste." The self's weakest self funnels batter as quickly as it can, into cakes. These are cut into round shapes resulting in a lot of wasted cake. I can wound myself too much. "The self's shrapnel rewounds the self. The self's wounds belong to and reinjure us all" (Suzanne Stein). I can bring anything in. Push it with anything. Even that written by the most hopeful, and not fighting, but if I am reading I am stumbling, I stumble and push it in, I fall upon anything because I am stumbling: "I've not been fond of the blog's tendency to group information chronologically, one of those structural arbitraries that seems to have influenced a generation—and they thought they were just being "new york school"—haha" (Joel Kuszai, Buffalo Poetics List, Dec. 7, 2005).

That there are wounded or ailing animals at the end of a poetry book and nobody talks about them. In a fur-skin coat I saw myself. Ailing. There was a superimposed face on my face and I gradually came to see my own belief that it could never change. In this way my face functioned as an image on film.

I am writing this so that I can read it to you in January. Thinking of you and how the light will be. Low, and nicely glowing. In a little over a month. We're assembled, moving forward like a comb. In time. With one of us is another of us. Inside the nest, that is a time of occupation. "A nest-and this we *understand* right away- is a precarious thing, and yet it sets us to *daydreaming of security*" (Gaston Bachelard). To say otherwise would be to deny everything I have seen and heard. On the computer, the radio, from the mouths of humans. "On a table / or bent towards her feet on the floor." I give up wanting to see for myself. But I still want to be with us, seeing the new duck, the one with a heathery purple head and breast. "Would a bird build its nest if it did not have its instinct for confidence in the world?" (Bachelard) This wanting to be with us at the lake. Walking around it talking.

I mistakenly think the message is from Electronic Poison Center. Just when I most needed my mouth to feel clean, celery was there for me. Whoop, that's it, living in the first world *for* you. Even if you don't want to recycle. Or do the real work. Forever Adjunct, little 21 throws the imitation stone tablets down from the top of miniature mountain. Her friends quail, and are terrified. "The terrified quail and want to know!" (David Larsen) As if everybody's object from everybody's narrative were available for play or distress. And so it was. What was done on the couch is done.

I keep thinking you know me and my relationship to sauce. *Tumultaneity.* I couldn't think it without thinking I must say it, suggest it. Thinking I must "make it so." Overwhelming compulsion. I meant a stream of images. A now dated word for the place where we sit together, side by side, watching the images go by. Now along with film there must be one of each. "Of what?" I thought later, and then captured my thought as speech. Desperately plotting one's steps forward, just to go forward, not understanding one's own behavior but needing to, "writing that keeps tumbling onto the page for lack of balance."

I can't believe it's working this time. Except for the days when it's not working. Boring fear that someone else has done it already better. Or recently *and* better. Geraldine Kim's variating margins. Because the day still exists in its container, is called day, then dailiness can't be over. I have to win the argument sometimes. Even if no one is arguing. How does one "embrace our volatility?" Is that what I've been waiting for in the we writing? Previously I required only movies. Now we and volatility. Because there is a we. And volatility, and day. So I asked the day to contain itself. Is it so hard to remain day. Even when felt differently. I'm stubborn. I stub my toe.

In each bite somewhat striving to make meaning. Oatmeal, agave nectar, cashews, soy milk. It is morning. I missed a day. Yesterday. When I ran into Robbie. Experiences I don't want to have but still "succeed" at. I was proud of building a method around broken file extensions. I do not know what a file extension is. When I don't know what's wrong with an application, I blame it on the file extensions. The surface, through sheers, stands there looking idyllic with raindrops all over its face. *Vertigo*. Everyday I think along with the cover of Jane Sprague's *fuck your pastoral*, "fuck your pastoral." Usually right as I'm sitting down, thinking about ducks I saw at the lake. Their duck legs. They look like two leaves attached to a duck body with something impossible, like soap. Peter Pan sitting on Wendy's bed, head in his hands, talking in a low voice about work. She is sewing something. Not him.

Later the same day. That I would have to continue. Which meant more reading, more irritation. My big project had all the usual things: anxiety, image, idea, institution. Movies, TV series on DVD sent through the mail, how is shame different from embarrassment. The anxiety of each. The image of each. Around its idea. Institutionalized. "You will have to give me a wedgie," I said to the text. Is there something which cannot be faked. A question from earlier this evening. That I have been coasting along for so long in my leather seat doesn't mean I could do it just anywhere. Coast along. A metaphor is always reductive but sometimes true, that leather seats, the kind for coasting on surfaces, could be identical structures repeated across very different sorts of vehicles. Vehicle of my first and second—omission—I learned that from him. "Every text is a received idea," she said. You will have to know it again and again if you are going to stay with me, "Everything that I have seen and felt is included" (Sei Sonagan).

"Don't look!" heard on the inside. So saying I went forward. Eating figs. Reading the book with a red cover while other ideas raced through my mind, my habit of reading so unlike hers, who re-reads some pages two or three times in a row and then records the ideas found there, both the book's and her own, on notecards. It is December. Almost. I am saving some things for another day. I am only recording the days as they go forward. And what goes into them. It is a memoir. Of what goes. And how it is going.

441-8729: insisting on its personhood. A numberal among the numberals. Insisting on the desire of its personhood, among the phones, insisting it represents. Of course I "run into" people unexpectedly on the street. Just not the people I want to. A footpath around the lake. Not the street. The hoax of a negating second clause. Everson, as evoked by Suzanne as we walked around the lake, on the hoax of form. On the footpath. We'd planned it. The walking. There's a big difference. I look up the quote from Everson later, in *Fulcrum*: "It is more the sort of form which Robert Lowell has been using, which, I suppose, is why I feel I can see through the hoax of his stuff." Everson was everywhere these days. I'd missed him. But now I had the *Fulcrum*, from Catherine. She gave it to me at breakfast. I am recording for specific numberals. They will get lost. ". .there is a demand by the publisher for the glittering line in a glittering poem—though they generally go together badly" (Landis Everson). I have not been doing "too much" at all. Not too much email. Not too much mail. I am waiting in the we writing to see. "I am always telling myself the narrative is still ok" (Aaron Kiely). Running side to side onto the page as paragraph, waiting for the glittering thing in the underbrush to appear, whiplash from a whip only, if I find a line here you can be sure I will investigate it. Some days are longer than others.

I should mention something cinematic every day. A moving image. "I do it on the daily" (Fergie). Some characters on the *L Word* become more narrow in the second season. More narrow physically. Also their hair curls, or straightens or is cut off. In the second season narrative widens, there's a delta, seen from above its tributaries narrow, move out in more directions, and the land between them will, we know but do not yet see, eventually become arid. On its way. Dry spots of muffled sex. Indicators. The women's bodies are narrower because the narrative is narrower in its widening way. Making room between their bodies for more bodies until the cumulative affect is felt in a collapsed plot.

All the moisture evaporates. Bodies stacked side by side and on top of each other, like husks. The characters who narrowed and then disappeared. There's a tan color in my mind. It is fall. "The bad days will end / because we will end them" (Dana Ward). May it be so of fall. The most beautiful I don't care.

Nothing but a very severe idea could separate them. They were so close. Needing a very severe idea to go their separate ways, if only for Saturday. *A very severe idea*, an appointment. The change in tense was a real change in time, the change in person a real change in her person. It was 3:20 in London, or outside London.

I guess I just never developed very good work habits. So the...to the...of anything else. A funny smell in the house. It's night. I wish this wasn't true. "OMG, OMG, OMG" (head in hands) "there's no structure." Boasting, "the most embarrassing thing I can think of." Is there always going to be recycling trauma. A banging noise coming from the garage.

Stubbing one's toe as a *demonstration*, hanging her head, "I'm so embarrassed." Which sort of gives you a nice stretch across the shoulders, it turns out. 5:18. Why don't we work until 5:30.

A sticker on the heater with instructions for what to do when the pilot light goes out. I know how to turn it on, and I know what to do when it goes out. You hope you'll remember to turn the knobs. Or someone will turn them for you. And you'll turn theirs. There's a stranger going in and out of the garage. The most embarrassing thing Woody Allen can think of. In a port wine reduction. With all this punctuation I hope I don't sound too much like Cynthia. Who I admire very much. And other things that might sound. Like I'm trying to sound. This boundary problem is my big appeal. A problem in some cases but not all. "How big is your dick?" "Average." Then I looked at my email. It was 5:28. Then I saved this as 11.23.05.doc. Then I looked at the file 11.20.05.doc. It was pretty embarrassing. It was prose. It looked like this:

Other people's knowledge was greater. Often it seemed that other people had more knowledge than I. Other people were greater. They knew more. Was it related? Bad in public but also in private, "What did she say?" I asked myself, and corrected myself. "Tell her to take it down!" Permeable, a lens stuck in one's face, a hushed tone. She got stuck in the tube and it looked then like her face was going to pop. No, she fell down the tube. Still, it felt as if her head might explode, or combust, or according to some established method fly into bits. Instead a single capillary on her nose very quietly burst. Talking about the other people, how they were greater, seemed to help. What they knew more about, mostly films and books. "Trivia," she'd dismiss their knowledge later, in private, on nights when she'd participated. She was dismissive, "Trivia!" on the nights when she couldn't. Participation. A trap. Other people having more knowledge.

A comforting thing enters, where you think about older ones who didn't get some of the knowledge at the same time as the others, they were too late, they were out of school by then, so when they read the knowledge it was by themselves and they read it "wrong."

That is how I'll do it.

Then the she-doll gets too excited. "Like an animal," I'd said about a friend I love, another poet, but it was more true of her-self. I am thinking I can get the money (boots) before she goes to New York.

Then there were sirens. I was 5:45.

*

November 11, 2005

6.1

"There you are, Therese," Dubois says to me, "free." Halfway up the
Boulevard.

Whatever the eye landed on.

Wasn't it... who said...
you have to start with a map, and not use all those dots?

The methods hover. It is hard to talk. The how to of satisfaction in open-
ing one's throat, and if there is harmony, it is accidental. A little crunk
falls out. It's not a competition. Who is most not cleaning house all the
time, waiting for dings of not-response.

"Have a look about—"
it's the only way

I could get to the party
and the only way
I could leave. The structure

is parallel. It is party. The only way
I am in this chair
little dings around my feet

and in my eyes. A misplaced
delicacy. That people could be in love
with love, like every Thursday

I go into the city

and lose you. Led back
to the foot of the scaffold.

Where you wait for something else
as the extinction of several species
pushes its way through the piecrust
and into your mouth.

So with this divot
and into this delve
do I pour my tears,
the height of autonomy.


6.2

Hey, look!
you *can* keep crawling around like this
I mean it's not ideal
but that part of the ego
has to go anyways

Whoosh
I flushed myself a letter down the toilet

I will tell you so many things
every day
like the internet
like nerve.com
like blogger
like the statue of Britney giving birth on all fours
it really did hurt me in private.

This paper in my mind
a bundle of nerves
at the base of the spine

another brain. The lower faculties. Sure,
my stomach is covered in fur—

I will count to nineteen and be done with it.

Things lodged in one's skin
saying go ahead to them
it's ok to leave me like this
on the table
it's ok to clean me out
which only produces more milk,
"ironically" the poem moves past
its objects come faster
and faster now, one really zips
around the lake at all hours

when I woke up saying I think
I am having a dental emergency

it happened at the lake
if it happened at all


6.3

Who's there?
I called out into the poem

no really
*who's there?*


6.4

In the morning, in the transfer of dish soap from one container to an-
other, function and use-value became overwhelmingly unclear. Was
this amber liquid, pouring from the mouth of a more utilitarian vessel,
intended to clean the smaller, more decorative container it entered at
a steady rate? Even if I understood the smaller vessel's being filled in

order to dispense I knew very little and thought for a moment to dip my finger in the stream and eat directly of the agent. As the delight of my confusion crept towards the patio it seemed I must investigate every model within this same sensation.

Each film provided a boundary and a gate against which I could push myself, as if against a human being, or an animal, or a mineral, or any other transitional object. Behind each gate was an antiquarian gate upon which I threw myself until my paws bled. Then we would play out these little scenes:

Well, do you want a yellow blazer?
Because I don't have one.

Me, verbal: you be too.

Who lived in a paint factory and so could not smell the paint.


6.5

Him, you, me, she. A place to live
and part of the formal workforce

I call for a ceasefire (august 3, 2006)

and
in and

a place to live


6.6

One of us is your listener. A landscape who adjusts her arm, or moves a piece of hair behind her ear, to better serve, this delve in a hill, a person with concave places where the language makes an imprint and bounces back. Don't get confused: a person is not a wax museum. A person is not a petroleum jelly museum. A person is not a rock-climbing museum.

Although you will get stronger if you keep sending messages. And every time they bounce back.

That's what I was thinking.

On a hunt of no small magnitude to not hear it.


6.7

having one of those moments
where otherwise we would have done it
exactly the same as before

walked up to the face
the statue presented
and gave it my best
Oh Geez, placed my head
in my hands
and once again
shook it from side to side
but this time really and truly
like a horse. Domesticated for labor.

I could not only not see
the moving vehicle
at any range
I could only run into it
with my upper legs. I had to
get worked up
into a state of agony or despair
or both. You can see
there was a lot of confusion
or go ahead, run into it yourself
but don't say "needlessly"
because I needed you
I need you there

rather than making it feel better
not to say, "that's easy to say"
but I am what I was, a federal agency
sitting here
deep in my heart
or walking across the room to you
my image in repose
installed in a mobile container
still willing to wait
in addition
my exacto knife
but also my best friend.

Rather than
making it better
I am going to sit here
slosh around full of coffee
and send your love
it is my love too
after all I am sending it
bouncing around the room
even the softest fabric
sends it back, the system
isn't really *all that*
closed, yet we wind up
as always
self-contained


6.8

and it was for this purpose, too
I called out into the poem
for a ceasefire

You shouldn't have any trouble understanding this, friends,
the idea of society *is* a powerful image
for you know, know ye not, or are ye ignorant, brethren,
in the beginning was emotion ...
Do you not know, brothers, I speak,
potent in its own right
I am speaking to them, men who know
Celine often repeated in his writings and interviews
the law, all the ins and outs the law hath,
this image has form
how that has authority over a man, dominion.
Reading him, one has the impression
how it works, and how its power only touches the living
that in the beginning was discomfort
as long as he lives
has external boundaries, margins, internal structure

For instance a wife
its outlines contain power to reward
the woman that has a husband
there is energy in its margins
bound by law
differentiated from chaos
but if he dies
this much is becoming known
if the husband be dead
for symbols
she is discharged
as incandescent, unbearable limit

So then if while the husband lives
no experience is too lowly
if she lives with another man
all in all, the most elaborate attempt
while her husband is living
she is called
how thresholds symbolize beginnings—
obviously she's an adulteress.
But if the husband die
his whole narrative stance seems uncontrolled
if her husband be dead
sighting the crest
though she be joined
why *does* the bridegroom carry his bride?
She is quite free to marry ·
the step, the beam, the doorposts
with no one's disapproval.

Wherefore my brothers
you also died, were made dead
where sense topples
to make a frame
through the body
which is a necessary everyday condition
that you might belong
entering a house
you might be joined
even to him
the way an animal is
free to marry
in half across the middle
bring forth fruit
for celebrating a truce
and this is something like what has taken place.

For when we were in
the flesh, excreta, breast milk, saliva

doing whatever we felt we could *get away with*
a thin film
aroused by the law
constantly threatened with bursting
at work in our bodies
with maximal stylistic intensity.

But now
the narrative yields
we are delivered
used as a diagram
wherein we were held
two extremes that moreover change places
so that we can serve in a new way
because the rituals work upon human flesh
and not in the oldness of the letter.

But I can hear you say then
according to the most exact calculations
if it was no longer entirely part of herself
if the law-code was bad as all that
is the law sincerity?
Its own independent life?
Certainly not!
Here in town, the law-code has a perfectly legitimate function
on his estate I would not have known
what sincerity was
that far from needing pity
had not the law said
he was very attractive
I would not have known what coveting was.
His uncommonly expressive face
dressed up to look like a virtue
and timid politeness to women
ruined my life.

Don't you remember how it was,
among the thousand things reflected there?
I do, perfectly well,
the place where that rose heap was on display
sincerity seized its opportunity
when I approached
found a way to pervert the command
which many another better man has
wrought in me
to handle and to smell
every kind of covetous desire
within a hedge
without all the paraphanelia of law—

compared to it, the perfume
sincerity looked pretty dull.

For I was alive apart from the law once
the year that followed was the saddest
but when the commandment came,
sincerity sprang to life
and I was fooled.

And the commandment which was social
ordained unto impression management
intended to cooperate, but
I found that discrepant roles developed.

For sincerity beguiled me
the library looked as she had pictured it
pretty much dead.

So then the law
had a fatalistic sense of itself
its good and common sense
being drawn from one wrong turning to another.

Did then that which is good become death?
Did the fact in itself still seem harmless enough?
Whose mind could be severely logical?
By no means.
They could be of use to each other
in order that sincerity,
a fertile source of harmful complications,
might become utterly sincere.

For we know that the law is spiritual
but I am carnal, dizziness, noises, buzzings, vomitings

for that which I do
on the rough seas of the English Channel
I do not understand
and not only as a metaphor
what I want to do
and even more so the sick body
I do not do
what I don't understand
is that often I seem to be worn out

and if I do there is no glory
what I do not want to do
is best for myself and then do it

one of literature's most abominable scenes

it becomes obvious
the law is—
as it is
a buzzing pain that rises
in the same neutral tone.

I realize that in me
that is my flesh
omitted the phrenological head

I have the desire to do good:
plates, pots, chairs and lamps
but I cannot carry it out.

My decisions, such as they are
don't result in tightly fastened bootstraps.
Now if I do what I do not want to do,
it is a vision
it is no longer I who do it
broken up by the rhythmic sound of the voice.
It is sincerity living in me
which prevents images from crystallizing
and gets the better of me every time
causing them to break out into sensation.

I find then the law that
could only offer a perverse negation
fainting spells....resentment...

for in my inner being
a delight in the law
dipping his pen into the inkwell
not all of me joins in that delight

touching the pages
our creation is that teacher
I see another law at work
and the duration of our life
stealing anguished glances
is that teacher
against the law of my mind
our trials and death is that teacher
wretched man that I am
there is always a teacher nearby
two feet on the fender
and there is the teacher beyond

who will rescue this body of death
at the doors
able to touch the economy
I offer all my efforts to that teacher

I've no place to begin, I click to agree with the software agreement for Mac OS X Security Update 2007-05, when did I become this way (person)? I'll drink two cups of tea. I'll eat five cookies in a row. That will be my project. I will do this every night at the same time. I'll read *The New Yorker* and highlight certain kinds of sentences and later these will become my project. I'll call it: I READ THE NEW YORKER. It will sound like this:

"With her long brown hair, flipped up at the ends, and her artfully fresh face, she looks like Marianne—"

"Ross was a slim, sporadically belligerent man in his early forties who had grown up in Novia Scotia..."

"In the bleak grayness of December Beijing, at the hotel where I had arranged to meet her, she struck a defiantly ethnic note..."

"He has a disarming, slightly gap-toothed smile and a trim gray chin-strap beard..."

"...a striking woman with a strong face and high cheekbones."

"A baby-faced guy from suburban Chicago..."

"Koons, who is fifty-two, looks very much the same as he did at thirty—"

"...although she looks fabulous in "Fay Grim," striding about in lingerie and long coat...she seems just too feathery to hold together a movie that is, in any case, on the verge of flying apart."

Are you my (mother, father, husband, project)?

Daylight Savings Time Update, QuickTime Update, Java for Mac OS X 10.3 Update 5.

Prompted since 2005 I didn't do them. Doesn't matter, placeholders, things rhyme—even when I don't "comply" or use that word—if something would only appear here I promise, promise not to remove it in order to sound more clean, to sound good—

About twenty-five years ago, Yvonne Rainer compiled a list called Shameful Conditions and Occurrences. This is that list.

"To live alone."

"To arrive at a social gathering alone."

"To go outside in clothing not suited to the weather."

"To say something that can
be traced to someone else."

"To have nowhere to
go on Saturday night."

MOLLY

"To have no interest
in Jacques Lacan."

"To have no friend
with a summer cottage."

"To have no family."

"To be dirty, to smell."

"To have no interest in people."

"To be gossiped about."

"To be sexually betrayed."

"To be ignorant of
current popular music."

"To be disloyal to a friend."

"To gossip."

"To become middle aged."

"To lose one's youthful beauty."

"To be enraged."

"To be inordinately ambitious."

"To have more money
than your friends."

"To have less money
than your friends."

"To not understand
what is said to you."

"To not recognize someone."

"To forget a name."

"To lose one's powers."

"To go down in the world."

"To have misfortune befall one."

"To be bored with one's friends."

"To be thought of as superior
to what one knows oneself to be."

"To discover what one thought
was common knowledge about
oneself is not so."

"To discover that closely
guarded information about
oneself is common knowledge."

"To have less knowledge than one's students."

If something would only appear, I promise, promise not to remove it in order to sound more clean, to sound good—

When I finally begin to trust in the persistence of relation, at least the one with you, which, as it turns out, is the only way I can imagine trusting anyone else, I'm in the car, beloved metaphor for communication, something breaks, I can't stand it, stuck between all these big dirty american cars, with their big dirty windshields and cigarette ashes in their beige posterior windows...posterior? Yes of course the car has an ass, it's a honda, ok it's me. Big dirty american car. Even when built in asia or europe, what's a jeep, anyway? I want to ram them.

The first tower of One Rincon Hill rises next to the bridge I started to say *slowly,*

isn't that how things change, or how it seemed to me, bi-weekly commuter in rush hour traffic to therapy on Divisadero between Bush and Pine.

Traffic tends to speed up right as I get close enough to see the foundation of the tower. I'm driving. I'm talking on the phone. I'm looking I can't see. Vaguely it's brown instead of glass, a pile of dirt with some scattered casings, what are casings, I must mean there's a lot of metal. And lax security, that can't be true.

I think someday I'll drive and then walk to the base of the tower in order to get a better look, like a novelist with enough resources might travel to or even live in the foreign setting of her next project. No, I already live there. In a basement studio. I wonder whether the building above me could withstand a major earthquake. That's a placeholder, I love the place I live, it's damp, I think it's structurally unsound.

When complete, the south tower of One Rincon Hill will be the tallest all-residential tower west of the Mississippi: 62 stories, 641 feet, 400 above previous zoning limits. The condos start at $500,000 running to 2.5 million. Only eight units in the South Tower remain unsold (June 20, 2007).

As part of a re-zoning deal, developers agreed to exceed the usual percentage of units the city requires residential developers sell at below-market rates or provide offsite. None of the affordable housing for One Rincon Hill has been or will be built onsite. The first location is in Bayview-Hunters Point, built in cooperation with a local church.

August 2005: construction of the south tower is delayed after the groundbreaking ceremony because inspectors have concerns about whether the tower could withstand a major earthquake. Nothing happens for six months.

July 5, 1934: The Battle of Rincon Hill. Police attack striking longshore workers on the San Francisco waterfront. Labor counters with a general strike lasting four days.

July 21, 2006: a metal construction deck collapses at the site. Two carpenters and two ironworkers are injured when they fall approximately 15 feet.

Are you my (brother, sister, therapist)?

When viewed from the bridge, from the bottom, while driving, the tower seems insecure. While talking on the phone, and full of rage, I think or say it looks like a pretty good target to me. So close to the bridge. I don't know what makes a good target. But it looks like one.

There was nothing when I started, friends, but now it smells, it's brown instead of glass, a pile of dirt, some scattered casings, my project has a rash, a wart on the bottom of its foot, a tendency to break out, severe cramping, a complex cyst on its left ovary. The tone seems Biblical, whenever I address my friends like that I sound to myself an awful lot like a pastor, an impostor who started with nothing, nothing but blackheads, "hard with feeling", drifting between persons, in a car on the bridge, on the phone. Not fighting. On the phone in the car. When I finally begin. I want to ram my car into another car.

The target everywhere comes into sight, broken parts, and no replacement, something weird, twisting on its stem, cutting off the blood supply

"She seems just too feathery to hold together"

"She comments frequently on her "bad behavior," as if a pocket spycam pursued her at all times" (Brian Kim Stefans)

she can't stop

you have to stop
your notes are a mess

who told me that
all of that
there, put it in a basket
with the others, this mess
is economic, it represents
the time I had

Alice Notley waiting on a dream
in order to start a long poem
me too
especially as it doesn't seem encouraged, as a practice

often I think
that if I just sit here
with these terrible feelings
I will be permitted to read
*The New Yorker*, David Sedaris
is a terrible person
show me where it isn't true
feelings ARE facts
round after round
roman candles bleeding into the months
before and after our local
national celebration, we understand
the first and also the last

foundation and only possible creator
crawling from the wood
begins with the same letter
of wherever it was hiding
in this beam
is my body
my baby but let's pretend
we're at a shower
playing that game
where you can't say war
now let's begin

TO GOSSIP                     WHAT'S WRONG WITH YOU

YOU *ARE* A PROGRAM                     TO DESTROY

# ALIBI OF A PULVERIZED DISCOURSE

IT *IS* A JPG     THAT CAN BE TRACED TO SOMEONE ELSE

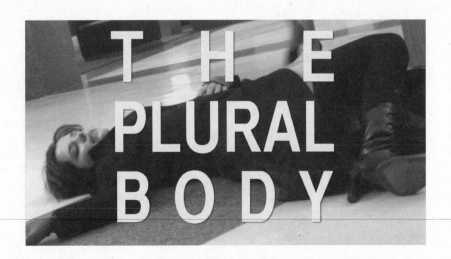

# THE PLURAL BODY

IN WHICH I WANT TO LOVE YOU BETTER

A SKIN WITHOUT PUNCTURE

HARD WITH FEELING
CLEANING THE HOUSE ON SATURDAY NIGHT

MIMESIS AND ALTERITY

SEX AND THE CITY          I HAVEN'T READ THAT BOOK

I HAVE NO FRIEND WITH A SUMMER COTTAGE
I AM VERY INTERESTED IN JACQUES LACAN

"NO, I INSIST"         THE IMAGE DOESN'T SUFFER

IT LIKES THE WAY IT LOOKS      ALONE IN THE ROOM

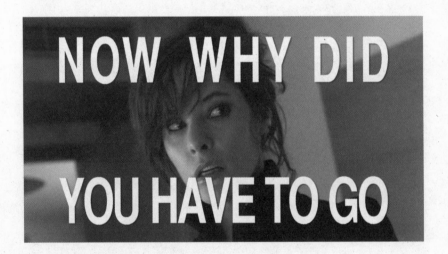

IT ISN'T A MATTER OF UNDERSTANDING

AND DO THAT TO YOUR EYE

WITH INTERNAL ORGANS    YOU CAN'T JUST TURN IT OFF

AS    A    CHILD
BENEATH THE GLASS

THE IMAGE MUST RETAIN ALL ITS PRECISION;

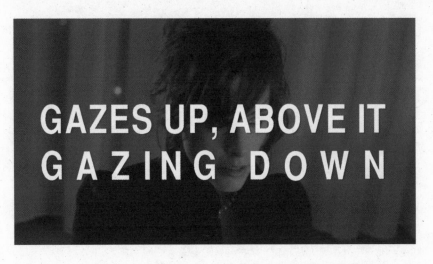

THIS MEANS THAT WE DELIBERATELY PRETEND
TO REMAIN WITHIN THIS CONSCIOUSNESS

AND PROCEED TO DISMANTLE IT, TO WEAKEN IT
TO BREAK IT DOWN ON THE SPOT

EVEN IF ONE DOES NOT

AS WE WOULD DO WITH A LUMP OF SUGAR BY STEEPING IT IN WATER.

SO THAT THE SERVER
KNOWS YOU ARE FINISHED

HENCE DECOMPOSITION IS HERE CONTRARY TO DESTRUCTION

IN ORDER TO DESTROY SOMETHING
WE SHOULD HAVE TO ABSENT OURSELVES FROM IT

AND SUCH EXTERIORITY IS POSSIBLE
ONLY IN A REVOLUTIONARY SITUATION

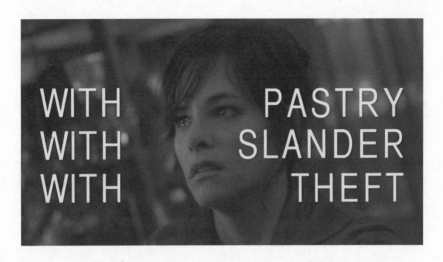

TO DESTROY WOULD ULTIMATELY COME TO NO MORE
THAN RECONSTITUTING A SITE OF SPEECH
WHOSE ONE CHARACTERISTIC WOULD BE EXTERIORITY

EXTERIOR AND MOTIONLESS:
IN OTHER WORDS, DOGMATIC LANGUAGE.

IN ORDER TO DESTROY, IN SHORT
WE MUST BE ABLE TO OVERLEAP.

BUT OVERLEAP WHERE? INTO WHAT LANGUAGE?
INTO WHICH SITE OF GOOD CONSCIENCE AND BAD FAITH?

WHEREAS BY DECOMPOSING
I AGREE TO ACCOMPANY SUCH DECOMPOSITION

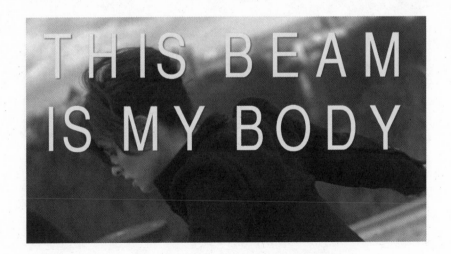

TO DECOMPOSE MYSELF AS WELL

# ON THE VERGE OF FLYING APART

IN THE PROCESS I SCRAPE, CATCH AND DRAG

00:00 - 00:51

*Audrey Hepburn sits alone at a patio table on the upper deck of a ski resort, eating lunch beneath a yellow umbrella. Pan across resort lunch crowd to facing umbrella, from which a hand emerges holding a gun. Cut to Hepburn about to take sip of her coffee. Cut to hand/gun, stream of water. Hepburn's face covered in water. Cringes. Pulls down sunglasses.*

Don't tell me you didn't know it was loaded—

Shit!

*blackout*

00:51 - 01:07

*sound: "99 Red Balloons" (Seven Seconds) into "Combat Baby" (Metric)*

01:07 - 1:44

*Scene opens on pile of dirt, construction materials in foreground. A bulldozer is partially visible behind the dirt. Palm trees, highrises and hotels in background. Red balloon floats above the dirt. Yang Kue Mei enters frame from right, walking on a dirt or partially paved path lined with flower boxes. Park in distance. She walks towards the trees on the horizon. Sound of birds, and her footsteps. She is wearing black heels, mini skirt, striped t-shirt and black blazer. Brownish bag over shoulder.*

the form I mean
it's loaded, it's spring
when I start writing this
in the green zone

it's Aspen in Dubai
in Colorado it snows
far into the season, it's unseasonable now
that *is* the season
silent, permanent, filmy horizon
over the horizon, another spring
inside the snow globe it won't stop snowing
or it won't snow
in a rolling blackout all year round—

"a place to discover earth friendly ideas and alternatives
compatible with the inland northwest lifestyle!"


01:45 – 02:27
*Cut to close up of Yang Kue Mei walking through the park. She is on the same
flower-box lined path/road. She walks. Sound of her footsteps.*

slow... down....                    *(film momentarily runs in reverse, Yang*
maybe not.... that slow          *Kue Mei appears to take a single step*
there you go                           *backwards then proceeds as before)*

who am I fighting?
the scene isn't from Hollywood
Tsai Ming-Liang is one of Taiwan's second new wave directors
think Ang Lee, but not
on English-language websites *Vive l'Amour* is often discusssed
in terms of its relation to European modernism, Antonioni
the long shot
the alienation
on the edge of the city
nothing gets to me
except when it does

the body: "when I heard the clacking of your heels"
or, reception: "I knew it wasn't a nurse"

02:27 - 03:58

*Yang Kue Mei turns the corner on the road and continues walking through the park. As she turns we see a green area of the park behind her that isn't under construction. The skyline from the opening shot now in the distance behind her. An expanse of dirt to her right. She passes puddles, construction material. More flower boxes line the path.*

*sound: of her footsteps is looped on top of itself once, and then again. Sound of shells / mortar dubbed over sound of footsteps towards end of section.*

it was spring in the green zone
in the feminine shade
guarded by a crazy quilt of personnel
on a clear April night, white plastic tables in the garden
fill up with an assortment of archetypes:
sniffed by dogs six times
bags sent through four metal detectors
photographed once by a body scanner
patted down too many times to count
and a bottomless barrel of pork
sausage for breakfast
hot dogs for lunch
pork chops for dinner
so many cases of beer and wine on the roof
that it began to bow inward
with polo shirts, golf balls and golf towels
a prominent official and one of his escorts
one of the guards
one person
a policeman
a student
a gunman
a rocket
a rocket launcher
the busdriver
the colonel

his driver
the scene?
a civilian car
a commercial centre
a security source
a university female student and a child
two bodies
two choppers
two armed men
two explosive charges
three people
four others
five machine guns
six suspects without outlining the nature of the charges
nine bodies handcuffed and blindfolded
18 treacherously killed martyrs in a cemetery in the suburbs of the city
255 elements dismissed
ripped through the cafeteria

*sound: voice of two soldiers dubbed over film "Damn...fucker...car bomb —car bomb—car bomb—let's go—let's go—there's gonna be another one"*


03:58 - 5:24
*Cut / pan out to view of trees, lampposts, skyline, Yang Kue Mei in the distance. She is walking on the same path, which in this section of the park has been recently tiled or bricked. A series of newly cobbled stairways and paths criss-cross the hill. There are other figures walking, jogging, working. A low grey building. Pan slowly left to the freeway running alongside the park. A worker crosses the hill with an orange coiled hose hung over his shoulder. Yang Kue Mei walking up the path.*

*sound: silence*

my image sometimes takes the form of a disoriented body
in which one part doesn't know what the other part is doing

something takes hold of you, where does it come from
what sense does it make?

in the effort to explain
I might be said to "have"
this seems so clearly the case

dramatizing my detachment is invoking it as an option
that might be true
that one has forgotten another person
but it can be so only because it was already
exhausted and does not know why
what that lover meant, or means to me
but that something else has come along to take its place
as if full substitutability were something for which we might strive
one's own knowing and choosing
might try to tell a story here
about what I am feeling is called into question

a story that grief is privatizing

as if one could invoke the protestant ethic
"oh I'll go through this way and that will be the result"
there is, as we know, but there is also
the ways I am gripped by each other
as something that often interrupts
an aim
a project

one cannot say "I'll apply myself"

I think one is hit

one does not always stay intact

05:24 -08:31

*Cut to Yang Kue Mei walking down into an area of the park with rows of wooden benches, perhaps part of an outdoor ampitheatre. A man with white hair and a brown coat is sitting on one of the benches, reading a newspaper. Looks with irritation over his shoulder in her direction as she enters. She sits down three benches behind him. Closeup of her face. She is crying. She stops crying and blows her nose. She smokes a cigarette. She cries.*

*sound: silence*

[Breathing, crying sounds, lighter, blow nose. Crying sounds. Breathing sounds, ending on an inhale.]

This work owes very particular debts of gratitude for the conversation, friendship, writing, thought, performance, generosity, feedback, presence and love of Del Ray Cross & the poem swap group, Dan Fisher, David Horton, Catherine Meng, Ronald Palmer, Cynthia Sailers, Juliana Spahr, Suzanne Stein, Konrad Steiner, Rodrigo Toscano, Dana Ward, Alli Warren and Clive Worsley.

Versions of this writing have appeared in *Mrs. Maybe, fascicle, EOAGH: a journal of the Arts, Plan B, War and Peace* vol. 3, *ANIMES, Ping Pong, Cypress Magazine, Effing Magazine* and *Rabbit Light Movies*. Thank you to the editors of these publications.

My practice of sometimes parenthetically listing the writer (but not volume or book title) of quoted material in the body of the text is directly influenced by Cynthia Sailers' practice of the same in her recent work.

Not all materials are attributed. Roland Barthes features prominently.

A much shorter version of "Chapters First through Third" was performed alongside a scene from *Aliens* (James Cameron) at the Poetry Center and Yerba Buena Center for the Arts in San Francisco, a *Viz. Inter-Arts* event in Santa Cruz, and a book release party at Teachers & Writers Collaborative in New York.

"Epistle Seven" was written for a group reading in celebration of *Vanitas* magazine and is seven minutes long when read aloud. All text is taken from the seventh chapter, book, or section of the Book of Romans (versions including King James, American Standard, New International, and Eugene Peterson's *The Message*), *Work* (Louisa May Alcott), *Purity and Danger* (Mary Douglas), *Madame Bovary* (Gustave Flaubert), *The Presentation of Self in Everyday Life* (Erving Goffman), *Powers of Horror* (Julia Kristeva), *The Romance of the Rose* (Guillaume de Lorris, tr. Harry W. Robbins), *Anna Karenina* (Leo Tolstoy) and *The House of Mirth* (Edith

Wharton) and the lines of a popular Bhajan (devotional chant) in English translation as presented by Katchie Ananda during Sunday Kirtan at 7th Heaven Yoga in Berkeley.

"The Image Record" (second iteration with images) was constructed in collaboration with Konrad Steiner for performance at New Yipes in July 2007. Sources include *Feelings Are Facts* (Yvonne Rainer) and *Fay Grim* (Hal Hartley). In performance, the text on pages 88-89 was accompanied by live navigation of Google maps street view. Although the south tower is now complete, the basic route as pictured in July 2007 can be re-traced (as of April 2008) by viewing the intersection of 2nd Street and Harrison in San Francisco and moving northeast on Harrison approximately four blocks, past the Sales Center for One Rincon Hill (look to your right), the 1st Street Bay Bridge on-ramp, and the construction site.

"Charade / Vive L'Amour" was performed at Artists' Television Access and Counterpulse in San Francisco, and the REDCAT theater in Los Angeles.

Stephanie Young lives and works in Oakland,
California. She's the author of *Telling the Future
Off* (Tougher Disguises, 2005) and she edited
the anthology *Bay Poetics* (Faux Press, 2006).
Recent editorial work includes the collabora-
tive website www.deepoakland.org. Find her
online: www.stephanieyoung.org/blog.